Kerikeri Mission
and Kororipo Pā

Kerikeri Mission and Kororipo Pā

An entwined history

ANGELA MIDDLETON

OTAGO

Published by Otago University Press
PO Box 56 / Level 1, 398 Cumberland Street
Dunedin, New Zealand
F: 64 3 479 8385
E: university.press@otago.ac.nz
W: www.otago.ac.nz/press

First published 2013

ISBN 978-1-877578-34-2

A catalogue record for this book is available from the National Library of New Zealand.

Publisher: Rachel Scott
Editor: Wendy Harrex
Design/layout: Fiona Moffat
Printed in New Zealand by Wickliffe (NZ) Ltd

Front cover: Detail of *L'Etablissement des Missionaires Anglais a Kidikidi – Nouvelle-Zelande*. Copy by Antoine Chazal of drawing by Jules Louis LeJeune. National Library of New Zealand Te Puna Mātauranga o Aotearoa, Alexander Turnbull Library, C-082-094

Contents

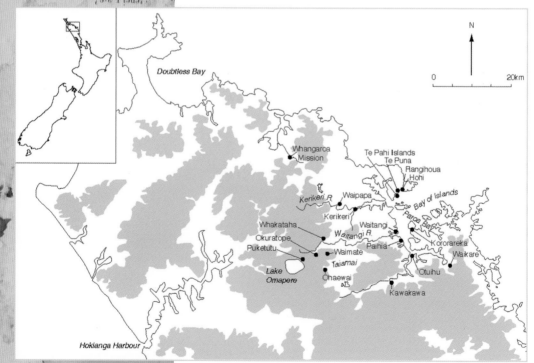

An enlarged version of this map appears on page 70

Entrance of the Bay of Islands, viewed from the south, painted during Augustus Earle's stay at Kororāreka, 1827–28.

The expansive, attractive harbour we now know as the Bay of Islands was given this name by James Cook in November 1769. It has long been a favoured place of occupation, beginning some eight hundred years ago with Māori settlement. The ancient Māori name for the Bay is Ipiripi, although its meaning is not clear.

Europeans found this harbour ideal and its land fertile when they began visiting in the late eighteenth and early nineteenth centuries. The Kerikeri River formed an important waterway providing access inland from the harbour and its maritime resources, as seasonal planting drew Māori and later, Europeans, away from the coast. The Kerikeri basin and Kororipo pā formed a significant gathering place for Māori before they set off on voyages to the south or the north; later this same pool of water and its backdrop of hills became the scene of an early Māori and European settlement, the Church Missionary Society (CMS) mission.

TIPPAHEE
a
NEW ZEALAND CHIEF

From an Original Drawing by G.P. Harris.

Te Pahi, engraving dated 1827 by
W. Archibald, after a drawing by
G.P. Harris, made during Te Pahi's visit to
Sydney in 1805.

National Library of New Zealand Te Puna Mātauranga o
Aotearoa, Alexander Turnbull Library, A-092-007

Samuel Marsden, c. 1832–38.
Lithograph after an oil painting by
Joseph Backler, a convict artist.

From P. Harvard-Williams, *Marsden and the New Zealand
Mission*, University of Otago Press, 1961

1. Kororipo Pā and Kerikeri Mission

Kerikeri today provides tangible evidence of the entwined history of Māori and Pākehā, the relationship that founded modern New Zealand. It is the site of New Zealand's oldest surviving European buildings, the most visible reminders of the CMS mission set up in 1819 on the Kerikeri River, while alongside these structures stands Kororipo pā and the remains of its kāinga, the territory of the paramount chief, Hongi Hika, under whose jurisdiction the mission was established. This book tells the story of that unique settlement and the people – Māori and Pākehā – who made it.

Kerikeri was not the country's first mission. That honour rests with the small, isolated valley of Hohi (also known as Oihi), located closer to the northern entrance of the Bay of Islands, under the eye of Rangihoua pā. At that significant site, no standing structures and little visible evidence remains. Kerikeri's story is more substantial and material.

Encounters between Māori and Europeans began in the last decades of the eighteenth century, most notably with the voyages of James Cook and of French explorers Jean François Marie de Surville and Marion du Fresne. Cook left European crops behind, as did the French. These exchanges became more frequent after a British convict colony was established in New South Wales in 1788. Few Europeans lived in the Bay of Islands until the early years of the nineteenth century, although there were ephemeral, impermanent settlements in the far south of New Zealand. By the last years of the century, the NSW governor, Philip King, had sent potatoes, pigs, goats and other goods to the Bay of Islands. These multiplied under the management of Māori such as the chief Te Pahi, who supplied provisions of pigs and potatoes to visiting ships on their way to the whaling and sealing grounds. For Māori, metal tools and nails were very desirable in return, as muskets were to become. As well as trade, a two-way traffic soon developed, as some Māori joined ships' crews and explored the wider world. Bay of Islands chiefs began to follow European knowledge back to its source, seeking new ideas and technology in order to maintain or increase their mana in the shifting alliances of the Māori tribal world.

Te Pahi, from Rangihoua and Te Puna in the northeastern part of the Bay of Islands, was the first influential chief to visit New South Wales. He and four sons stayed with Governor Philip King for three months in 1805, and were presented with tools, livestock and plants when they returned to Te Puna in early 1806. King also sent a kitset wooden house that the ship's carpenter erected for the chief on his island, just offshore near Te Puna. In Port Jackson, Te Pahi also met the colony's chaplain, Samuel Marsden. These two became firm friends; Marsden considered the chief 'a man of high rank and influence in his own country. He possessed a clear, strong and comprehensive mind, and was anxious to gain what knowledge he could of our laws and customs', inspiring Marsden to return to England to gather resources for the first Christian mission to Maori, to be established under Te Pahi's protection. This early contact was lost, however, when Te Pahi died in 1810.

Te Pahi's younger relative, Ruatara, also met Marsden in Port Jackson in 1805. He became a crew member on a whaler, and later travelled to England in an attempt to meet George III (which he was prevented from doing). When Marsden boarded the *Ann* on his return voyage from England to Port Jackson in 1809, he was amazed to find Ruatara also on board, ill from mistreatment and coughing blood. Under the care of Marsden and the missionaries he had just recruited for the New Zealand mission, Ruatara returned to good health. He subsequently stayed with the chaplain on his farm in Parramatta for some months, learning about wheat-growing, flour-making and other agricultural techniques, intending to develop this technology in the Bay of Islands. Ruatara finally returned to Rangihoua in 1812, where he became Te Pahi's successor.

Although the mission was delayed by the news of Te Pahi's death, Marsden continued his preparations. After an initial exploratory voyage in March 1814 to consult with Ruatara and other chiefs, Marsden and his 'mechanic' missionaries sailed again on the *Active,* arriving in the Bay in December 1814. The new settlement, established under Ruatara's protection, at Hohi alongside Rangihoua pā, consisted of carpenter William Hall, shoemaker and 'twine spinner' John King, Thomas Kendall the schoolmaster, and their families, as well as 'ticket-of-leave' convict labourers, a total of some twenty-five European men, women and children. The 'mechanic' missionaries were men who had a practical trade qualification but were not ordained. They came as 'lay catechists'. While the mission was Marsden's brainchild, he did not stay in New Zealand but returned to his Parramatta home in March 1815.

This first mission, established in December 1814, struggled as conflict escalated between the mission settlers. The site was

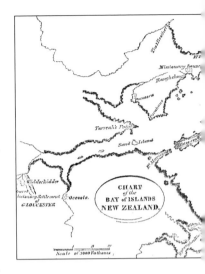

Detail of 'Chart of the Bay of Islands' from the *Missionary Register,* 1822. Top right is the Hohi mission ('Missionary houses') next to Rangihoua pā ('Ranghehoo'). On the far left is the Kerikeri ('Kiddeekiddee') mission ('Missionary Settlement of Gloucester'). Waitangi ('Wytanghee') is at the bottom. Immediately to the right of Kerikeri is the village of Ōkura ('Occoolo'). In the enlarged version of this map on page 71, Kororāreka ('Corroraddica', now Russell) is on the peninsula at centre.

problematic, being situated on a steep hillside with little flat land suitable for growing food. The small settlement was dependent on initial help from Ruatara, but the chief sickened and died in March 1815, only days after Marsden had returned to New South Wales. Marsden, however, insisted that this was the spot for the mission, overlooked and protected by Rangihoua and its chiefs. At times, as food supplies ran perilously low, the mission settlers looked anxiously for the *Active*'s return with flour, sugar and other essentials. Sometimes it was months before they saw the ship return to Hohi from Port Jackson.

With Ruatara's death, the renowned Ngāpuhi warrior Hongi Hika became more prominent in the Bay of Islands. His base was twofold: Kororipo pā on the Kerikeri River, where he shared control with his close relative and ally Rewa (from the hapū Ngāi Tāwake / Te Patukeha), and the food-producing lands and forests inland at Te Waimate, associated with Ōkuratope pā. Hongi's gardens also extended into the Te Puna area. He and his people moved between locations according to the seasons. Kororipo, also known as 'the deliberating place of chiefs', was an important meeting place for rangatira, a place where political issues could be debated. War parties gathered there to discuss strategies and plan campaigns before undergoing ritual preparations for battle. After leaving Kororipo, any departing fleet would collect other waka as it carried on through the Bay and southwards. Hongi's Point, at the far edge of the pā, was the tapu place to which the taua returned from warfare, where rituals to remove tapu from warriors and the dead took place. Although small, Kororipo's fortifications protected any inhabitants from assault, and served as the coastal bastion of the fertile inland areas of Waimate.

THE KERIKERI MISSION

By 1819 Marsden had decided the Bay of Islands mission needed to expand in numbers and activities, with a new settlement close to good agricultural land and easier access to timber for building. Rangatira throughout the Bay were keen, even desperate, to have a missionary settle amongst them, for missionaries would bring European goods (including guns), trade, schooling and political advantages. Hongi Hika saw there would be material benefits if the mission were to be at Kerikeri. In 1819, his pā and village offered the promise of better fortune and prosperity to the CMS missionaries, as well as the hope of conversions of its Māori occupants to Christianity.

The Kerikeri River formed a 'grand highway' to the sea for inland Bay of Islands Māori, the emerging Ngāpuhi iwi. Marsden had first come to Kerikeri in early 1815, on his way inland to

Waimate with Hongi, to see the chief's inland territory. As he travelled up the Kerikeri River from the harbour, a turn around a sharp promontory suddenly revealed a basin beyond which a narrower section of the river continued. Hongi brought Marsden here again in 1819, as the most suitable place for the new mission. The promontory itself, formed into the defences of Kororipo pā, was the stronghold of his people. Further up the ridge, back towards and overlooking the mission site, was the kāinga, or village (perhaps known as Kirikōkai). Mission visitors in 1824 noted that this village consisted of about sixty huts, along with other traditional structures such as whata (storage platforms) and racks for drying fish.

Samuel Marsden arrived in New Zealand for the second time on 12 August 1819. Travelling with him were the Reverend John Butler with his wife Hannah, nineteen-year-old son Samuel and two-year-old daughter, also Hannah; James Kemp (a missionary blacksmith) and his wife Charlotte; Francis Hall (who was to be storekeeper); and carpenters – William Puckey, William Fairburn and William Bean and their families. Marsden also brought three horses destined for Kerikeri, as well as cattle and bullocks (as he had at Hohi).

Five days after their arrival (they stayed at Hohi), William Hall (missionary carpenter), Francis Hall, Butler and Marsden travelled with Hongi in his war canoe to the Kerikeri River to select the site for the new mission, now planned as the principal CMS settlement in the Bay of Islands. Marsden hoped the Kerikeri site, with its flat, fertile land, would become the centre for grain and food production for the two mission stations. Before the party left Kerikeri on the following day, they marked out the location of a store to hold CMS goods and arranged with Hongi for his men to build this and temporary accommodation, a raupo structure, for the carpenters.

Hongi Hika had brought the CMS mission to Kerikeri, closer to the centre of the Māori population in the Bay and to his own inland food-growing territory of Waimate. It would be subject to him and Rewa, as Hohi was to the rangatira of Rangihoua. The land the two chiefs sold to Marsden at Kerikeri amounted to 13,000 acres for which, according to the purchase deed, Marsden handed over forty-eight axes. However, John Butler noted that Marsden also provided Hongi and Rewa with gunpowder: an item Marsden himself had strictly forbidden being traded. And there was a wooden house that William Hall started building for Hongi on the approach to Kororipo pā, although it was not completed until 1824. While axes and gunpowder sealed the deal, Kerikeri Māori also understood that they would now have their own Europeans in exchange for the use of the land.

Aerial view showing Kerikeri locations.

Plan of Kororipo pā and the kāinga, with the mission buildings at the top.

Reproduced from Simon Best, *Kerikeri Basin National Heritage Area Archaeological Survey*, 2003, p.16, with thanks to the author

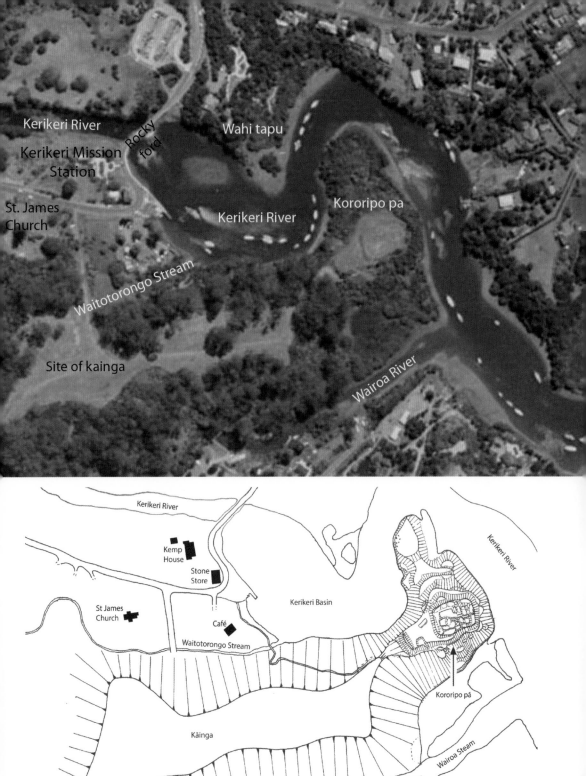

Kerikeri River
Kerikeri Mission Station
Rocky ford
Wahi tapu
St. James Church
Kerikeri River
Kororipo pa
Waitotorongo Stream
Site of kainga
Wairoa River

Kerikeri River
Kemp House
Stone Store
Kerikeri River
St James Church
Café
Kerikeri Basin
Waitotorongo Stream
Kororipo pā
Kāinga
Wairoa Steam
N
0   150 m

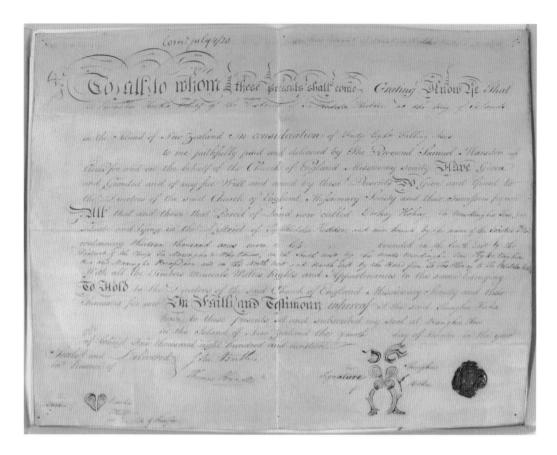

The deed of sale for the Kerikeri land was not signed until 4 November 1819. Hongi's co-signatory was Rewa. Kendall and Butler signed for the CMS, while Hongi and Rewa signed with their moko. There is no official mention of Marsden's contribution of gunpowder; no doubt this was a private exchange, away from the sight of other missionaries. Having completed the land purchase, Samuel Marsden returned to his base at Parramatta, in New South Wales.

Well before the deed was signed and Marsden's departure, work had begun on the new mission. William Hall built a punt to row large quantities of timber and other materials the nine or ten miles from Hohi up the harbour to Kerikeri. The first mission building was the raupo structure, where the carpenters Bean and Fairburn briefly stayed. A sawpit was dug, where Māori sawed timber into boards. The second structure was a wooden 'house for the working natives to sleep in' – Māori who had come from Rangihoua. More buildings – a blacksmith shop, measuring 21 feet by 15 feet, along with a weatherboard store, 60 feet by 15 feet – were quickly under way. On 12 October 1819 Marsden remarked on the seedlings that had come up, the grape vines (planted by

Mete Rewa. A sketch copied by J.F. Mann from an original portrait drawn by G.K. Mann during Rewa's visit to Sydney in 1831.

himself) in leaf and the many fruit trees planted. Also by this date, Butler and William Hall had chosen a spot for a church, 'on top of a small eminence'. This first chapel/school building was not erected until 1824, on a site later obliterated by a road to the shore.

A party that included missionary wives Charlotte Kemp and Hannah Butler went up to Kerikeri from Hohi on 9 December 1819 to see their new home; they shifted there some ten days later. Hannah Butler and Charlotte Kemp were apparently 'much pleased with the new settlement', although this sentiment may not have lasted long. The store, with an earth floor, was completed in late December, partitioned into temporary accommodation for the Butlers, their servant Richard Russell, the Fairburns, Beans and Puckeys. This first store would remain in use until the Stone Store was completed some sixteen years later. By then, it was quite rotten. The Kemps and Francis Hall moved into the blacksmith's shop.

Supplies were punted to Kerikeri, where they were issued to families from the new store by storekeeper Francis Hall. Building continued into the New Year, with carpenters Puckey and Fairburn erecting outhouses and fences, seen as necessary 'to keep off the natives from ye doors as much as we can'. Of course 'natives' were very much present in the settlement: four pairs of sawyers from the kāinga were 'constantly employed sawing Timber' and the Māori brickmaker George, who had learnt his trade at Parramatta, was making bricks with two or three assistants. Māori from Rangihoua also worked there for some time, until endemic conflict with the Kerikeri hapū led to their departure.

By mid January 1820, thirty of Hongi's people were employed breaking up ground in preparation for planting the first wheat crop. They received rations of ten pounds of potatoes and one or two pounds of pork per day. Other people were burning charcoal for Kemp, the blacksmith. In February, a house was started for the Kemps and Francis Hall. The toil continued, bringing sawn timber and logs in the leaking punt, built with no 'oakum, pitch nor tar'. Cattle and pigs were also transported in this unreliable vessel. Sometimes Kerikeri Māori and people from elsewhere, such as the rangatira Tāreha from Te Tī (and Waimate), helped with transportation, bringing war canoes to Rangihoua to carry goods back to the store.

Reverend John Butler helped with fencing around the buildings but confessed that he was not a good carpenter. The chimney he and the 'servant' Richard Russell built in two days at the end of January was not the best as they had no bricklayer. Only some of the men chosen for the mission were 'mechanics' or tradesmen; those who were not practical people struggled with such tasks. Butler recorded that this new fireplace was where

The deed of sale for the Kerikeri land, 4 November 1819. Rewa's moko is at the left-hand corner, Hongi's at the right.

Hocken Collections Uare Taoka o Hākena, University of Otago, S12-598c.

Mrs. Butler has four natives to cook for daily, besides our own family; and all our native sawyers, farmers, brick-makers, wood cutters, etc, are served daily from our place, as well as all pigs killed and salted, for the use of the settlement, and as Mrs. Butler has a young child, and no female (except a native girl) to assist her, to say the least, she is a complete slave to the concern.

Richard Russell apparently worked as a domestic servant too, killing the pigs for salting and serving food to Māori workers.

The Kerikeri mission became the hub of the society's operations in the Bay of Islands. Butler was the schoolmaster at Kerikeri and was appointed superintendent of both the Kerikeri and Hohi missions, in effect replacing Thomas Kendall as leader. (Kendall had formed a close alliance with Hongi, coming under disapproval from the missionary brethren for this and other misdeeds.) Of the families who arrived at Kerikeri in 1819, the Kemps were to prove the enduring occupants, beginning an association with the place that lasted into the later twentieth century.

Butler had Hongi, Tāreha and Rewa to dine with him in early December 1819 and afterwards the chiefs and their men camped around the house. This kind of exchange with rangatira became regular and frequent. He gave Hongi a pair of shoes as his feet were badly chapped, and thought 'he should be clothed, as he is our principal chief'. In the same month, Tāreha's sick brother stayed a fortnight with the Butlers. Others were 'on the sick list' while Mrs Butler made them 'rice, tea and other nourishing things'.

Marsden arrived back in the Bay of Islands on 27 February 1820, bringing with him a 'pious young man', James Shepherd, who was to be stationed at Ōkura, some distance from Kerikeri, where Te Morenga was chief. As with his previous visits, Marsden soon left (with Te Morenga) to reconnoitre other parts of the northern North Island, sailing in the *Coromandel* to the Hauraki Gulf and the 'Thames' area. From there, he walked to both Tauranga and the Waitemata with Te Morenga.

On his arrival, Marsden was dismayed to find that Kendall and Hongi, with Hongi's younger relative Waikato from Rangihoua, were planning to travel to England. The group were working on an orthography of the Māori language, following on from Kendall's first book in Māori, and wanted to complete the new book they had been working on – *A Grammar and Vocabulary of the Language of New Zealand* – and have it printed in England. Kendall also wanted to receive full ordination, while Hongi was keen to meet King George IV, whom he considered a rangatira like himself. The amassing of arms may also have been part of Hongi's agenda.

Hongi's departure in March 1820 was 'much lamented' as it would leave the Kerikeri settlement vulnerable to attack on all

Rev. Yate's drawing of Kerikeri viewed from Kororipo pā, published as a lithograph in 1835. Although a fanciful representation of the mission structures, some details are accurate. It shows the Stone Store alongside the mission house (not completed at the time it was published), the 1829 chapel on the hill and the Baker house on the hill next to it (only a single-storey building, not two as shown). The structure in front of the store may be stonemason William Parrott's shelter. Clarke's first bridge across the Waitotorongo Stream can be seen at left. The stage for the hākari display on the hill above is quite unrealistic and the original mission structures, including the store, have been hidden behind vegetation.

Plan of Kerikeri showing pā, kāinga and mission structures, including those built in 1819 / 1820. The site of the 'old store' (9) now lies partially under the restaurant opposite the Stone Store; the Kemps' original house (10) is likely to be the 'smithy' that still stands next to the restaurant. Redrawn from Kempthorne's 1843 survey plan, OLC 39. Scale is approximate only.

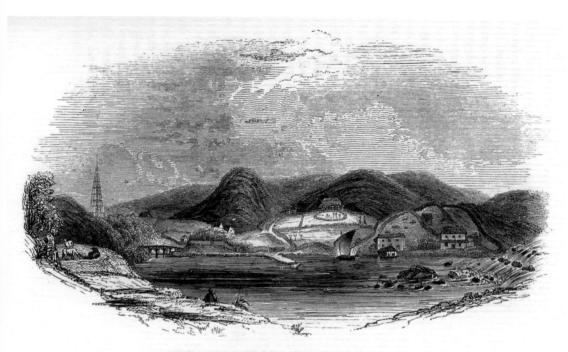

KERIKERI SETTLEMENT, WITH A STAGE ERECTED FOR A FEAST.

Page 172.

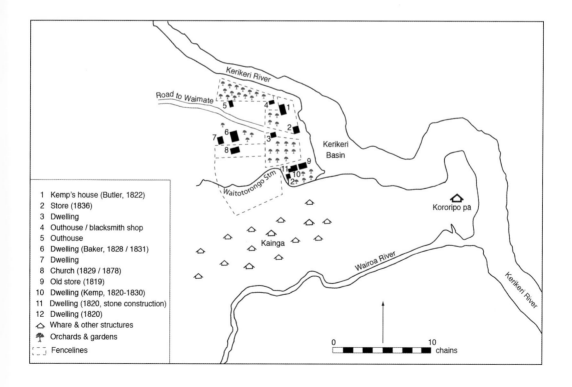

1 Kemp's house (Butler, 1822)
2 Store (1836)
3 Dwelling
4 Outhouse / blacksmith shop
5 Outhouse
6 Dwelling (Baker, 1828 / 1831)
7 Dwelling
8 Church (1829 / 1878)
9 Old store (1819)
10 Dwelling (Kemp, 1820-1830)
11 Dwelling (1820, stone construction)
12 Dwelling (1820)
⌂ Whare & other structures
🌴 Orchards & gardens
⌐⌐⌐ Fencelines

sides, without the protection of the paramount chief. Richard Cruise of the *Dromedary*, the ship that had brought Marsden to the Bay of Islands, pointed out that the missions were dependent on the precarious protection of the chiefs, and in particular Hongi; moreover, although they had been established for six years, 'not a convert had yet been made'.

After Kendall and Hongi's party arrived in England, a meeting with the king was arranged, at which George IV and Hongi exchanged pleasantries and discussed matters, including apparently their domestic lives: George IV was then embroiled in a divorce from his wife, Queen Caroline. Hongi expressed surprise that while he lived with several wives, King George could not manage one. Gifts from the King included a helmet and gun for Waikato and a coat of chain mail and two guns for Hongi, who amassed further arms – some three hundred muskets and powder – in Sydney on his way back to the Bay of Islands. This journey contributed to Kendall's alienation from the CMS brethren and he was suspended from the society and finally dismissed in late 1823 for a number of reasons, including adultery. More positively, he succeeded in completing the grammar and having it printed, and it was subsequently used in the mission's schools. Meanwhile, soon after their return in July 1821, Hongi set off at the head of a war party of combined Ngāpuhi men, armed with the new muskets. This was the beginning of the 'musket wars', a phenomenon that continued into the 1830s as northern Māori took retribution on enemies to the south.

Although Kerikeri may have appeared an isolated outpost of European settlement at the end of the second decade of the nineteenth century, it was actually a place of much coming and going. Boats and waka travelled backwards and forwards from Rangihoua, Hohi, Paroa Bay, Kororāreka and places in between. Missionaries and Māori walked to the inland settlements of Waimate and Taiamai, where food was purchased and people were visited, sometimes with medicines or simply tea and sugar for the sick, or other particular requests. Missionary wives exchanged occasional visits between Rangihoua and Kerikeri. Supplies from NSW and England arrived on board ships moored in the Te Puna inlet and further out in the harbour. Days were spent rowing these supplies in the mission's boat up the Kerikeri Inlet to the store, from which they were then issued to individual families at Hohi and Kerikeri.

Visiting ships also brought irregular but very desirable letters from family and the Church Missionary Society in England, keeping up a correspondence that often took well over a year or even two for letters to be exchanged. At Kerikeri, the routines of monthly prayer and quarterly committee meetings were

TAUA MURU

The 'Town of Gloucester', as John Butler called the new settlement, was quickly brought to heel. Its place within the Māori world was soon established when it was subjected to a taua muru, a plundering party taking ritual confiscation, as Hohi's had also been. This set the context for the mission families for the coming years and placed them under the control of the iwi and hapū who had mana whenua. Equally, they were subject to attack from those outside the area who had a grievance. In November 1819, the Kerikeri settlement was plundered by Te Morenga and men of Ngāre Hauata/Te Urikapana from inland Bay of Islands, who had been in dispute with Hongi and Rewa over cockles taken from tapu ground (one episode in an ongoing conflict). The two groups had long been enemies. Damage to the mission was not major: tools were taken from the blacksmith shop, pigsties were destroyed and pigs taken. The mission was viewed as Hongi's: plundering it was a legitimate way of dealing with a dispute over matters of tapu. Or, possibly, Te Morenga and his men carried out the plunder to express their anger that Hongi had succeeded in bringing the missionaries into his own territory.

Hongi Hika (centre), Waikato (left)
and Kendall in London, December
1820. An oil painting by James Barry,
commissioned by the CMS.

National Library of New Zealand Te Mātauranga o Aotearoa,
Alexander Turnbull Library, G-618

followed. Morning, afternoon or evening schools were held in the
settlement houses, often in Butler's house, with fifteen or twenty
Māori reported to attend. The orchards and gardens were worked,
as increasing areas of wheat and oats were put into cultivation
with the intention of making the mission independent of the CMS
for more of its food requirements – as Marsden had long expected
it to be.

The first children of Kerikeri missionary families were born
in the early years of the settlement. William and Sarah Fairburn's
eldest son, Richard, was born in March 1820 and their daughter,
Elizabeth, in August 1821. Charlotte Kemp gave birth to her
second child, Henry Tacy Kemp, in January 1821; her first baby
had been stillborn, born at Hohi in 1819. And the first of James
and Harriet Shepherd's twelve children was born at Kerikeri in
December 1821; tempted by the women at Ōkura, James Shepherd
had returned briefly to Port Jackson to marry in 1821, before
coming back to live at Kerikeri, where he applied himself to the
study of the Māori language, writing hymns and translating the
New Testament. He was also the mission horticulturalist.

At the distant edge of a European frontier, missionary wives
maintained households that attempted to demonstrate the

standards of civilised domesticity, the ideal of a Christian family. As part of this cultural raft, appropriate standards of appearance and domesticity were maintained. Women's clothing was stitched by hand, embroidered and ironed. 'Domestic training' was part of the schooling offered by the missionary wives to girls and women from the kāinga. Needlework skills were taught to missionary daughters, and to Māori women and girls. Māori, adults and children, joined the missionary households. Food was cooked in iron pots over open fires and households of numerous people shared a basic diet of pork and potatoes, the pork sometimes being replaced with beef.

By 1821 there were over fifty 'settlers' at the 'Town of Gloucester'. Tāreha, the Ngāti Rēhia chief from Te Tī, visited Butler in May, staying to dinner and breakfast. He came again with some of his family in June. In the same week, Hongi's eldest son Charles (also known as Hare Hongi) was brought to Kerikeri, badly burned in a gunpowder explosion. He remained at the mission for some time. Butler's 'foreman' at this time was 'Tyewangeh', also known as David Taiwhanga, who later became the second Māori convert to Christianity at the Paihia mission. Butler had engaged Taiwhanga soon after he arrived at Kerikeri and commended him as a man of 'quick discernment' who 'learns everything very fast'; he considered Taiwhanga a 'flywheel in the machine, which puts every other cog in motion'. It was through him that so much farming, gardening and fencing had been accomplished in a short time at Kerikeri, as well as the felling and towing of timber. Butler paid him 'an axe a month for his labour' and provided him with European clothing. The payment of an axe was standard exchange for a month's work at this time.

Daily life at the Kerikeri mission was interspersed with what might be termed 'intercultural exchanges and clashes' as missionaries, subject to the larger Māori population of the kāinga, protested against traditional Māori practices and tried to subvert them. Missionaries continued to attribute events, whether negative or positive, to divine intervention, the mysterious 'hand of God' operating to ensure the success of their plans to convert Māori 'heathen' to Christianity. Against this background, the 'musket wars' were well under way: taua were leaving from Kerikeri (and Rangihoua) and returning months or even years later, bringing prisoners from the south. The returns of the fighting parties were dreaded, as scenes of murder and cannibalism followed, carried out at Hongi's Point, near the far end of Kororipo pā. At such times mission families rescued slaves where they could, taking them into their own households and families. Utu, or recompense, was usually paid to chiefs for these people.

Tareha to the Life, 1844. A watercolour
and ink drawing by William Bambridge.

W.C. Cotton journals, Dixson Library, State Library of NSW,
Vol. VIII, p.24a

In early 1822 Hongi and others returned from a war expedition to the 'River Thames' and Waikato. Butler reported that many of the war captives were killed within sight of the mission. Mrs Butler gave 'two axes for a half-caste child' said to be the son of the doctor of the *Coromandel*, a ship that had visited the area in 1820. He was the youngest of four children taken into the household at this time. The Butlers were now settled into their new mission house, built between June 1821 and February 1822 (see Chapter 3). Chiefly children – one of Hongi's daughters and one of Rewa's daughters (aged about seven in March 1823) – also joined the Butler household.

John Butler had played a short role as the mission's first ordained minister and the superintendent of the two CMS missions at Kerikeri and Hohi. But, almost from the beginning, he was unpopular with other missionaries and his relationship with Marsden began to fall to pieces. Underlying the events of daily life, schisms within the mission deepened. The settlers – missionaries and labourers – quibbled over supplies, rations and the amount of their salaries, unsurprisingly, given the poverty in which they lived. Small details of daily life appeared to provoke conflicts. Francis Hall may have found the life of a missionary in the Bay of Islands too much. In June 1822 he gave up his role as storekeeper

HANNAH BUTLER'S WORKLOAD

In 1821 Hannah Butler was cooking food for eighteen Māori sawyers and farmers, as well as family members. She was 'almost worked off her legs', remarked her husband, but they helped each other and managed 'the best we can'. John Butler and Hannah Hitchman had married in 1798, when John Butler was aged only seventeen. They lived in Paddington, London, where Butler worked as a clerk in a carrying company until he was ordained in 1818 in preparation for his missionary career with the CMS. A year later, Hannah Butler found herself in the Bay of Islands, committed to a life in a kind of slab hut, confounded by the realities of tapu and utu (ideas of which she had no concept) and confronted with episodes of violence.

We know little about her thoughts and experiences, apart from the occasional comment by her husband about her endless industry at Kerikeri. We do know that she rescued young children brought back as slaves by fighting parties, making them part of her household, and that she took medicines and food to the sick at the kāinga. Although her role was similar to that of many missionary wives, her life differed in that she had only two surviving children, Samuel and Hannah (the Butlers' first son had died in infancy), while, for example, Charlotte Kemp had nine children and Martha Clarke, fifteen. John Butler considered his wife rendered completely 'wretched' by the conditions she had to cook in, in 'a little shed' he had built for the purpose; 'other women', he thought, 'were sitting at home in comfortable houses with little to do'. Butler must have been thinking of England, and only of the well-to-do.

and returned to England later that year, leaving behind the set of four mahogany dining chairs that he had brought with him in 1819. The Bean family also departed in 1822.

Samuel Marsden arrived on his fourth visit to New Zealand in early August 1823. He brought major changes, delivering Kendall's letter of dismissal from the society, while new arrivals came with him: Henry and Marianne Williams and their three children, William and Sarah Fairburn (returning from a visit to Port Jackson) and new Wesleyan missionaries. The Williams and Fairburns were destined for a new mission settlement at Paihia, but stayed with Kerikeri families until temporary homes were built there. The Wesleyans went on to Whangaroa, north of the Bay of Islands, to establish the first Wesleyan mission.

Although Kendall by now had moved away from the mission, his alliance with Hongi often brought him to Kerikeri, where he was not welcomed by Butler or the other missionaries. Marsden was also at odds with Kendall, and with Hongi. While Marsden attempted to leave the Bay of Islands in September, taking Kendall and his family with him to Port Jackson, the ship they sailed on, the *Brampton*, went aground on a reef in the Bay. Marsden was reluctantly detained for some weeks, while Kendall went back to his old home near Kororāreka and refused to leave again. Marsden's gift to Hongi of a 'European-style' house, which he ordered to be built for Hongi in October 1823, may have been an effort to win back some of the chief's favour. The house, located near the tihi (platform) of Kororipo pā (see Kempthorne plan, page 17) was completed in mid-1824. It may have been intended as compensation for Kendall's expulsion from the mission, as well as an ongoing payment for the Kerikeri mission's land and its protection, or perhaps it was a chiefly gift between chiefs. Marsden had long intended such a house to be built for Hongi.

Marsden could see relations between Butler and Kendall had deteriorated to the point where they couldn't both remain in the Bay of Islands, 'as there is manifest a spirit of hatred against one each other'. During this hiatus before he could find another ship to take him back to Port Jackson, the conflict between Marsden and Butler escalated. Finally, Marsden demanded Butler's resignation from the mission on what Butler considered a trumped-up charge of being intoxicated on board a ship in the Bay. Although Butler refuted this, as did others who were with him, Marsden insisted that he resign. Butler had no choice and on 14 November 1823 he and his family, accompanied by David Taiwhanga, embarked on a dismal sixteen-day voyage to New South Wales, in company with Marsden. From there, the Butlers returned to Britain, although apparently New Zealand kept a hold over them. John, Hannah and their daughter Hannah returned, arriving in Wellington in 1840 as New Zealand Company settlers. Their son Samuel Butler settled on the Hokianga, where he was drowned in 1836.

After this departure the Kemp, Shepherd and Puckey families remained at Kerikeri, along with the stockman, William Spikeman (Spickman). In late 1823 the two William Puckeys, father and son, began construction of Hongi's house at Kororipo, and the first chapel, which would double as the schoolroom, situated in the 'senter of the settlement and in a public situation'. James Kemp worked as blacksmith and storekeeper, issuing supplies to mission families and trade goods to Māori, or in payment for their labour. He and Shepherd attempted to expand the mission's wheat plantations, but self-sufficiency seemed impossible. The two missionaries found life hectic as they taught schools and tried to convert Māori and manage their daily secular affairs, including growing food. Hongi continued to dominate the mission and attempted to bring Kendall and his family to live there, closer to him. This would not happen.

The establishment of the Paihia station brought further changes in the Bay as the mission population expanded and the social circle was enlarged, extending to the Wesleyans now living to the north near Whangaroa. Meetings rotated between all three stations in the Bay: Hohi, Kerikeri and Paihia. The next year would bring new missionary blood to Kerikeri, as described in Chapter 3.

RULES FOR THE SETTLEMENT

In 1820, the 'Rules for the Settlement' detailed weekly provisions issued from the mission store.

For every man
8 lbs Flour
5 lbs of Salt Pork or 7 lbs of Fresh meat
1 lb of Sugar
2 oz Tea & 1/4 lb Soap

For every Woman
8 lbs Flour
4 lbs of Salt Pork or 6 lbs of Fresh meat
1 lb of Sugar, 2 oz of Tea & 1/4 lb Soap

And for every Child
4 lbs Flour
4 lbs of Salt Pork or 5 lbs of Fresh Meat
1 lb Sugar, 1 ounce of Tea & 2 oz of Soap

The allowances of food listed in the Rules for Settlement were for everyone living within mission households, including Māori and European workers. The superintendent could increase the provisions if it seemed necessary. Whale oil and lamp cotton for lighting were included in quarterly rations, as well as very large quantities of salt or saltpetre, which were required for preserving casks of beef and pork.

Missionaries were to obey the superintendent's directions 'according to their several offices, Trades and calling, and shall account to him for all their labour and time'. Each person (or family) permanently engaged by the society was entitled to a house, yard and garden to be cultivated 'for their private individual benefit'. No member of the mission was allowed to acquire or hold any private property, other than that granted by the CMS. No private trade was to be undertaken with Māori or with any ships, except for the 'general account and benefit of the mission'. All stores, including goods acquired from Māori (such as additional food supplies) or from any other sources, were to be deposited in the mission store and distributed to those engaged in the mission 'according to their wants'. The rations provided according to these rules were minimal, said to have been the same quantity as convicts were allowed in Sydney at that time.

2. The First Kerikeri Store, 1819

The first store at Kerikeri provided both storage for goods and temporary accommodation for missionary families until they had constructed their own dwellings. It is visible in the drawings of the mission by Rev. Richard Taylor on page 56 and was a weatherboard building, constructed by workers from the kāinga in late 1819. When Francis Hall gave up storekeeping in July 1822 and returned to England, blacksmith James Kemp, a 'pious, admirable and judicious man', took over a role he was to maintain for more than twenty years.

The accounts Kemp kept at the store are a window on daily life at Hohi, Kerikeri and other missions, as the CMS presence in the Bay of Islands expanded. The accounts were kept in two books: the journal or 'Day Book', roughly recording items as they were issued to people, and a ledger book into which these items were later transcribed under headings for provisions, 'cloathing' and ironmongery (this last category including tools and hardware). From about 1830, the ledgers for all three categories were collapsed into one, with headings for all the goods the store supplied at that time continuing across seven pages. Kemp wrote to either Parramatta or the CMS in London to requisition goods, returning copies of the accounts to the society's quarterly meetings in the Bay of Islands, as well as to Marsden in Parramatta and the CMS committee in London. The Kerikeri store also supplied the Wesleyans at Whangaroa with occasional supplies; the price for these was noted in the ledgers and the CMS was then paid on account in London. Individuals, such as ship captains and the secular settler Thomas Hansen, who lived at Hohi and then Te Puna, also purchased occasional goods from the store.

'An Account of Stores Issued from the Societys Store Kiddee Kiddee': the cover of James Kemp's account book, July 1822–January 1825.

Missionary families could purchase personal requirements – such as clothing, fabric and other items – from the store on their private accounts, with the cost being deducted from their salaries by the CMS. Other goods were issued for 'public service', to exchange with Māori for food and services such as building or labour. At the quarterly CMS meetings, each missionary submitted an account of the number of trade items (axes, hoes, spades, iron pots etc) they had on hand, showing how these had been 'expended' (in exchange 'for pigs, for potatoes, for general work … To purchase a canoe and sundry other things').

Kemp's first Day Book entry on 17 July 1822 records the stores on hand when he took over from Francis Hall. These included a large number of tools, among them 123 broad axes, 284 felling axes, 265,593 nails, over 1200 files, 140 sickles, nearly 1500 fishhooks and 4775 lbs of iron for the blacksmith's use. Items issued that day included one axe to pay for potatoes 'for the Natives', four hoes and one axe for 'Natives on the Boat to R Hoo' (Rangihoua), other tools dispensed for public service, and a knife paid to the 'Goat Boy', who worked as the goat herd. Fishhooks and axes were supplied to Captain Munro. 'Tohoo, James Kemp's Man' was paid one felling axe for a month's work, while the rangatira 'Tarriah' (Tāreha) received a gift of one iron pot. In August, 'Mr. Shunghee' (Hongi) received a gift of one adze, and 'Moca' (Moka) was paid one felling axe for the damage done to his potatoes by the mission cows. Perhaps as part of the same incident, Rewa was given a chisel, a 'gift for preventing Moca from shooting the cows'. Other gifts of tools included an adze to 'Ahehee' (Hihi) and to 'Tahiaree' (likely to be Tāreha again), two pocket knives and, two days later, one pair of scissors. The mission used 4500 nails in the same month, 23 files and 200 fishhooks, all of which were likely to have been as payment for small items or, in the case of the fishhooks, as rewards for school attendance. Some gifts may also have been part of an exchange for Māori artefacts. Kemp's letters regularly note taonga or 'curios' sent back to England, although the accounts do not record the purchase of such things. These included woven items described as mats, as well as shells, mere and greenstone objects.

In early March 1823 the ship *Endeavour* arrived with industrial quantities of 'ironmongery' goods. Kemp recorded receiving the popular fishhooks, along with clothing and regular food supplies. A chest of medicines was also noted, the main ingredients of this being castor oil, rhubarb oil, 'Bassilicon' and a case of 'white ointment'. 'Bassilicon', or more properly basilicum, is a traditional 'drawing' ointment composed of beeswax, pitch, pine resin and other oils.

Kemp's first account book, showing entries copied over from the Day Book, July–August 1822.

Collection of Kerikeri Mission Station © New Zealand Historic Places Trust Pouhere Taonga

Right: Page 1 of Kemp's 1822 'Day Book'.

Left and right: The store supplied axes and hatchets for many purposes: two mortising axe heads, also known as post axes.

Only hand-wrought nails were available in the store until the late 1830s or early 1840s, when cut nails were first imported. Wire (modern) nails did not come into common use in the Bay of Islands until the 1870s. These nails from the Stone Store show wrought (left) and cut (right) examples. Collection of Kerikeri Mission Station © New Zealand Historic Places Trust Pouhere Taonga, XSS.655 (left), XSS.656 (right)

Below: The first two of four pages in the Day Book listing goods received from the *Endeavour* on 10 March 1823. The goods included nearly 23,000 fishhooks, over 1000 hoes, 693 'falling Axes', 299 broad axes, 720 pairs of scissors, along with numerous adzes, files, knives, nails and horse harness. Collection of Kerikeri Mission Station © New Zealand Historic Places Trust Pouhere Taonga, MS1122(6) XKH.902

Large box from Kemp House with James Kemp's name carved into the wood. The 'No. 9' refers to a cask number and may be that on the *Endeavour's* list of goods received into the store.

Collection of Kerikeri Mission Station © New Zealand Historic Places Trust Pouhere Taonga, XKH.2631

Medicine chest, possibly that received in 1823, and other apothecary equipment.

Collection of Kerikeri Mission Station © New Zealand Historic Places Trust Pouhere Taonga

Large quantities of goods were regularly brought in on ships from Port Jackson and London. They had to be of good quality: Māori would not be fooled into buying poor tools. Kemp requested the CMS in London not to send 'unsound' tools as Māori refused to buy a particular brand of axe made from poor quality metal: 'the Natives are becoming very particular and they know a good tool as well as I do so that I should advise always to send good articles'. Hatchets were very desirable, popular not only as 'an instrument of war' but also for 'cutting down small wood' and clearing ground. Blankets, iron pots and axes were 'sometimes wanted', but hatchets were always asked for, and of one particular shape.

Gifts and payments for services continued throughout this first period from July 1822 to the end of 1824, when Kemp's first ledger account book ends. 'Peter & Engari' were paid with an adze each for sawing three logs. Unnamed Māori were paid in tools for a variety of services, such as rowing a boat to Rangihoua and back, searching for wild cattle, and bringing the stores up to Kerikeri from ships anchored in the deeper part of the harbour, closer to Paihia. Māori 'female servants' were likely to be paid an axe for three months' work, while Māori men were paid at the much better rate of one axe for a month's work, as were the 'goat boy' and the 'cow boy', who usually received a hoe or an axe for each month. Five men rowed Francis Hall's luggage to a waiting ship when he left Kerikeri in December 1822 and were paid a very good rate of a felling axe each for this one job. 'Mr. Shunghee' continued to receive regular gifts, sometimes twice in a month; in January 1823 he was given ten sickles, perhaps to harvest the wheat crop he and Rewa had planted at Waimate. Broad and felling axes or an iron pot were also regular gifts to him, as well as large quantities of clothing. These gifts, plus the house that Marsden had built for him, were a major expense for the CMS and suggest that the mission at Kerikeri remained very much within Hongi's fiefdom.

Not everything that left the store was a trade item or gifted. In February 1823, Kemp recorded the loss of fifteen axes, a hoe, seven adzes and six knives, 'stolen by the Natives going to Mr. Kendalls'. However, by the time of the entry for 1 April, Kendall had returned these tools. In July 1823, Kemp noted again, 'In the Night some Natives Stolen out of the Store', taking axes, adzes and hoes.

Despite the large quantities of goods arriving in the store, providing for the community's needs was not straightforward. In December 1824, little bread could be made as the supply of wheat had nearly run out. To add to the mission's troubles, a poor harvest was expected, as the soil was becoming exhausted from continuous cropping. Tea and soap were running out, peas and

Hatchet or toki patiti. This toki, of the kind used for trade at the store, has been made into a personal weapon, with the addition of a bone (possibly whale) handle, the knob of which has a hole drilled for suspension from a cord.

From the Bedggood family collection, thanks to Gavin Bedggood corn, issued (from 1824 onwards) in place of wheat, were nearly all gone and only a few pounds of rice were left in the store. Kemp was about to issue arrowroot in place of flour. Cornmeal was needed to feed the school children, as they preferred this and it was cheapest. A year later, the wheat crop looked much better, promising to provide enough for the settlement for the year, but soap and salt were all gone, and the 'Ironmongery trade getting low, Hatchets, Plane Irons, Scissors & Knives all expended'.

The Clarkes and Kemps were the only two mission families at this time and the wheat crop did provide enough for them. Hongi, Hihi and Rewa were still growing wheat at Waimate and traded it with the mission. Rice was dispensed on a regular basis, as was vinegar and 'biscuit', often given to the schools at Hohi and Kerikeri or paid to Māori for bringing up stores from the ships. Wine (possibly communion wine) was included in the ledgers at the end of 1823, when five gallons were supplied to James Shepherd. Equally large quantities of wine went to Henry Williams and George Clarke in 1824, along with gallons of 'porter'. In the three years from 1822 to 1825, however, little changed in the provisions received by the missions. In 1825, large quantities of 'Jews harps' came into the store, Henry Williams and John King each receiving seventy-two of these to distribute for 'public service'. And blankets began to increase in popularity as the preferred trade item: these, too, had to be of good quality.

Kemp's first entries for 'Cloathing' are quite sparse, compared with later lists of items provided by the CMS store. In August 1822, columns in the ledgers are headed 'Duck frocks, Striped Cotton Trowsers, Rugs, Worsted, Girls Bonnets, Striped Sherting, Stout Printed Stripe, Print not stout, Duck Trowsers'. Duck is a strong un-twilled linen or cotton fabric (canvas) used especially for outer clothing, as well as for small sails. Duck frocks were a labourer's shirt or smock, a traditional English garment simply constructed from rectangles and squares and gathered (usually smocked) onto the collar or a yoke. These garments were worn for both work and leisure: those for festive events, such as weddings, featured more elaborate embroidery. 'Worsted' was a woollen fabric with a straight weave. By late 1823, further fabrics were included, such as 'Single coloured print', 'Cambric', 'Calico', 'Dungaree' (denim) and more striped fabrics. Items favoured as gifts to chiefs like Hongi and Rewa, or as exchange for services provided by Māori from the kāinga, were: blankets; red, striped or check shirts; blue jackets; and blue and striped trousers. Black and white cotton thread and silk thread (for embroidery), along with 'Markin Canvas' and 'Shert', and 'Mettle' buttons also appeared in the ledger, the thread being supplied by weight in pounds and ounces.

Iron pots, known as 'goashores', are still in the Stone Store in 2013. A leg on this example has broken off.

Collection of Kerikeri Mission Station © New Zealand Historic Places Trust Pouhere Taonga

Wearing caps and blankets typical of stock from the Kerikeri mission store: Hakiro (Tāreha's son, who was baptised at Kerikeri in 1842), 'Nene Waka', and Rewa, April 1845.

W.C. Cotton journals. Dixson Library, State Library of NSW, Vol. IX, p.77a

Some new items of clothing and different fabrics arrived in 1824: ivory combs, hair brushes and 'Scotch caps'. Shifts, the only ready-made item for girls and women, appeared for the first time at the end of 1825; seventy-six of these were supplied to the store. They must have been popular, as nearly all mission families received at least a dozen. Women's clothing at this time was many-layered. It began with the shift (or chemise), a loose garment of about knee length, followed by corset and petticoat(s), and finally the gown. Additional items were possible, such as the tippet (a cape covering the shoulders), the fichu (a similar item, a triangular piece of fabric covering the shoulders), or an apron for working in. A pocket was worn as a separate item, attached around the waist. Knee-length drawers, tied at the back with an open seam from front to back, may have been worn underneath all of these layers, although these were originally an item of male clothing and were considered 'extremely immodest' when first worn by women at the beginning of the nineteenth century. This restraint appears to be confirmed by the accounts, as 'Drawers' do not appear until about 1836. As women's clothing was all hand sewn and not available ready made, as men's was, the store accounts show that large amounts of fabric were dispensed to missionaries for Māori girls and women.

James Kemp sent private orders from the mission families to England for some clothing items and large numbers of pairs of shoes. In 1825, he ordered twelve pairs of 'strong Shoes' for each of them, along with a pattern of both his and Charlotte's feet for size, as well as two dozen pairs of children's shoes 'from two years old to ten' (by 1835, they had eight children) and one dozen 'gray strong cotton stockings mans size'. In the same letter he enclosed a similar order for George and Martha Clarke, for twelve pairs of 'strong shoes' each, along with flannel, hat wire and 500 needles.

NIGHT SCENE IN NEW-ZEALAND.

Night Scene in New Zealand. Wearing a greatcoat and cap, probably from the store, James Kemp preaches at a Bay of Islands village.

Missionary Register, 1837

He asked that these things be forwarded to the mission by a whaler 'coming direct to New Zealand', as they required them as soon as possible, but they would have been lucky to receive them within a year. Kemp also sent a 'Native War [Weapon]' as a token of his regard. Other orders for private goods went to Port Jackson, where on one occasion Kemp requested the purchase of hops, wine, 'Hollands', vinegar, and enough fabric to make a pair of trousers. With this order, he enclosed some black cloth 'to make a coat and Vescote' (waistcoat).

Some say that rules are made to be broken. This was certainly the case for the CMS brethren. Despite the idealistic, almost socialist, requirement that missionaries should not hold any private property or undertake any private trade with shipping or with Māori, such trade certainly took place. Alongside the transparent store accounts, a black market operated, primarily in guns, the most desirable trade item for Māori, who would often provide pigs and potatoes only in exchange for muskets and not for any of the so-called legitimate goods from the store. This was especially the case when there were many ships in the harbour wanting provisions and the market price went up, or changed. The musket trade proved a source of conflict between the mission brethren, particularly for those at Hohi, where Kendall was exposed as a major operator in this trade and the blacksmith once attempted to shoot him with a pistol. Even Marsden's inclusion of gunpowder in the Kerikeri land deal transgressed his own rules on trading in arms. But the numerous toki, or hatchets, a legitimate trade item for the Kerikeri store, were equally useful as weapons, as the one illustrated on page 30 shows. This was an unavoidable trafficking in arms.

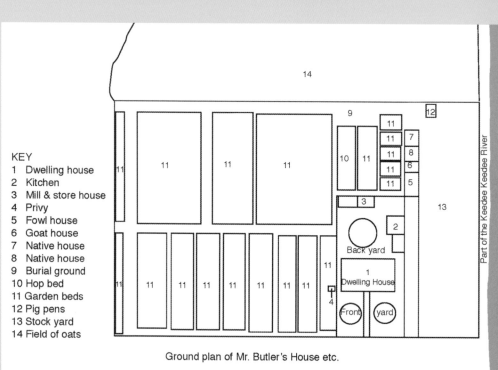

KEY
1 Dwelling house
2 Kitchen
3 Mill & store house
4 Privy
5 Fowl house
6 Goat house
7 Native house
8 Native house
9 Burial ground
10 Hop bed
11 Garden beds
12 Pig pens
13 Stock yard
14 Field of oats

14

9

12

11
11 7
11 8
10 11 11 6
11 5

3

13

2

Back yard

11

1
Dwelling House

4

Front   yard

Part of the Keedee Keedee River

Ground plan of Mr. Butler's House etc.

3. The Kerikeri Mission House, 1822

The dwelling houses occupied by the Kerikeri missionaries after their arrival in 1819 were rudimentary, and a more permanent building was needed to serve as the mission house. Early in 1821, John Butler, William Hall, James Kemp and the carpenters travelled inland to Kahikatearoa (Waipapa) to begin felling timber (mainly kauri, but some kahikatea and puriri) for a new house, which would be occupied by the Butlers. The logs were floated down the Kerikeri River to the mission, where sawyers cut them into boards. Carpenters William Bean and William Fairburn began work on the house in June, with Butler hoping it would be finished in six months.

The hope was almost realised. At the beginning of February 1822, the Butlers moved into the rather grand new house (now known as Kemp House), although it was not quite completed (Butler was still 'white washing and painting' the new mission house in February 1823). A celebratory dinner party took place, with missionaries and a ship's captain attending. Mrs Butler's work conditions must have momentarily improved; although the kitchen of this house was in a separate structure outside, it was adjacent to the main building. A year later, at the end of January

The parlour/chapel in the mission house, where Marianne Williams and her children slept in August 1823. The mahogany chair beside the table is one of the set left by Francis Hall. Collection of Kerikeri Mission Station © New Zealand Historic Places Trust Pouhere Taonga

1823, she and her husband celebrated a 'harvest feast' with the 'poor natives' who had been reaping the mission's crops. There were four large plum puddings, and a 'hog'. They all sat down to table, where Māori were confronted with the etiquette of an English dinner. Butler carved for everyone and Mrs Butler 'was waiting maid'. The guests left with many thanks, as well as payment in tools for their services in the fields.

After Henry and Marianne Williams arrived in the Bay of Islands with Marsden in August 1823, Marianne stayed at Kerikeri for some six weeks. She was relieved to see the English-looking Kemp and Butler houses (in contrast to Hongi's 'rude palace') as they were rowed around the promontory of Kororipo pā in the Kerikeri River. The mission house was painted white, and lined with wood inside. On her first night there, after the children were asleep, Marianne went to meet the Kemps in their cottage. She found a friend in Charlotte 'at the first interview' and everything in their compact, pretty house was 'as neat as wax'. The Williams' first dinner 'on the shore of Newzealand', at the mission house, consisted of 'soup, fish, ham, vegetables and pudding'. Some days later, Charlotte Kemp prepared dinner, described by Marianne as 'excellent Norfolk fare', for thirteen adults and nine children.

Meanwhile, Mrs Butler schooled Marianne on the management of pigs, poultry and rabbits. The Kemps' cow had plenty of milk,

David (Rawiri) Taiwhanga and a young woman, 'Etinou', were drawn by Jules Louis LeJeune in April 1824, on board *La Coquille*. These copies of his two ink

A washing tub, once lined with zinc, with a 'plunger' that was inserted in the hole in the top.

Collection of Kerikeri Mission Station © New Zealand Historic Places Trust Pouhere Taonga

drawings were made by Antoine Chazal in 1825 or 1826.

National Library of New Zealand Te Puna Mātauranga o Aotearoa, Alexander Turnbull Library, C-082-100

which produced excellent butter, but the Butlers' milk came from their goat. Goats were also used to pull carts, loaded with various goods or small children. Marianne was impressed by James Shepherd's ability to speak the Māori language, but considered the 'state of the natives deplorable'; Rewa's head wife had recently killed her own child, while a 'servant', Jane, had herself killed two prisoners brought back with a war party from the south. Mrs Butler arranged for two Māori women, one the Butlers' own servant and the other the Kemps', to wash the Williams' linen. These women were paid every three months, with either a hoe or an axe.

Henry Williams was in Paihia, working on the construction of the new mission buildings there, including their first house, the raupo 'Beehive'. Marianne and their children remained at Kerikeri, where the children began 'long neglected' lessons and were rewarded after a day's schooling by play with the Kemp children. As she was expecting another child, Marianne was not allowed to do heavy work. Instead, she took up her needle and thread to help Mrs Butler with sewing. While she may have enjoyed her sojourn at Kerikeri, it must have been complicated by the difficult CMS politics and John Butler's forced resignation from the society. It was only shortly after Marianne and the children moved to Paihia that the Butlers left Kerikeri to return to New South Wales.

After the Butlers had departed, for a few months the mission community consisted of the Kemps, the Puckeys and the Shepherds, along with herdsman William Spikeman. James Shepherd and his wife Harriet moved into the empty mission house, but they were not to enjoy its comforts for long. The Puckeys moved on to Paihia in mid-1824, but soon after were dismissed for drunkenness. Their son continued in the society's employment.

Francis Hall's replacement, George Clarke, arrived in April 1824, with his wife Martha and their young son George, on the French corvette *La Coquille*. Although he had once been a gunsmith, George Clarke came to the Bay as a teacher, and the Clarkes were to join the Kerikeri mission and live in the mission house. Clarke and James Kemp were childhood friends from Norfolk and came from a network linking evangelists to Parramatta and back to Britain. From 1824 until 1830, when the Clarkes moved to the new Waimate mission inland, they and the Kemps forged close links, forming the core of the Kerikeri mission. These links continued into the next generation when their children intermarried. Also on board *La Coquille* was Taiwhanga, returning to New Zealand after some months in New South Wales with the Butlers. John Butler had given him gifts of clothing, tools and soap; when he left the Butler house in Sydney, Taiwhanga 'cried very much'.

The Shepherd family was reluctant to leave the mission house,

but after orders from the committee they vacated it and the Clarkes moved in in May 1824. Almost immediately, Clarke (as schoolmaster) and others went inland to Waimate and Taiamai, where the larger part of the Māori population lived, to 'collect children for the school'. These included the sons of Hongi and Rewa. The emphasis in lessons was on literacy in Māori and useful skills. The students lived at the mission station and included both adults and children. They came from all the districts where Kerikeri hapū had interests. At the school, the boys were taught in the mornings, and the girls in the afternoons, while there was an adult school five nights a week.

Sunday services were held in the first small church (completed in 1824), but Clarke was initially shocked by the congregation's ridicule of Kemp's service in Māori, possibly prompted by his inadequate knowledge of the language. Some burst into laughter, others lay down and slept during the services. Kemp visited the kāinga regularly, as well as other villages around the inlet and as far away as the coast to the north of the Bay, but he often complained that people were inattentive towards his conversation on religion. The missionaries continued their regular visits inland to the Waimate and Taiamai districts, preaching and catechising 'in their imperfect Māori'. The missionaries' monthly prayer meetings and quarterly committee meetings, lasting one or even two days, rotated between Kerikeri, Hohi and Paihia. Missionary

women and children exchanged visits, staying with each other or assisting at births.

These events were cast against a larger backdrop of the movement of war parties, under the command of Hongi, Rewa and other rangatira, continuing their episodic departures from Kororipo and their returns, months later, with war prisoners. Culture clashes continued to occur when missionaries offended against Māori protocols of tapu and were subject to plundering, or when they complained about goods and food stolen for no apparent cause.

Seasonal tasks, such as planting potatoes and kūmara in the spring and harvesting in late summer, created times when the Māori population left their coastal settlements almost abandoned for inland plantations. At these times, the school was close to empty. In January 1825, records show that some of the school children had returned again after a hiatus in 1824, a common theme as different seasonal and traditional events interrupted Clarke and Kemp's imposed routines. Martha Clarke had six Māori girls living with her in the household; ten or twelve girls attended the afternoon school, where she and Charlotte Kemp taught reading, writing and needlework. The Kemps had about six boys and five girls living with them in 1825, with Mrs Kemp 'endeavouring' to teach the girls the domestic arts. One of the girls, then aged about eight, was Hongi's youngest daughter.

LeJeune also drew the Kerikeri mission station. *L'Etablissement des Missionaires Anglais a Kidikidi – Nouvelle-Zelande;* this copy of his original drawing was made in 1826 by Antoine Chazal. Note the size of the kāinga on the ridge at the left.

National Library of New Zealand Te Puna Mātauranga o Aotearoa, Alexander Turnbull Library, C-082-094

TAMIHANGA MAITARAHANGA, known as Tutu, is said to have been rescued during the musket wars by James Kemp and William Fairburn when he was a 'very small baby'. He worked as a gardener for the Kemps into the tenure of the Kemps' granddaughters, Gertrude and Charlotte, who 'loved' Tutu, 'extolled all his virtues and felt at a loss without him': the hoe (left) is identified as his and may be the one on his left in the portrait. St James Church records show that he was buried on 19 January 1904.

Collection of Kerikeri Mission Station © New Zealand Historic Places Trust Pouhere Taonga, XKH.2219/1-3, XKH.586 (hoe)

While Hongi remained opposed to Christianity, he treated the missionaries 'very kind' and with great respect, but still sought only muskets and gunpowder.

New missionary families came to Kerikeri from time to time, staying there before moving on. The Hamlins arrived on 25 March 1826 and moved into the mission house with the Clarkes, temporarily, as Mrs Hamlin was 'expecting to be confined very soon'. In January 1828, William Yate joined the Kerikeri settlement, and initially lived with the Clarkes in the mission house. In June, the Baker family followed. This brought the number of missionaries at Kerikeri to five. The Bakers moved in with the Kemps for three months, until a raupo whare for them was completed at the end of September. It was a trying time in a small house for Kemp, and he was unable to keep his regular journal for several months.

More permanent wooden houses may have been some time away; in March 1830, Hamlin, Baker and Yate were all still living in raupo houses. A wooden house was built for the Bakers near the church, but by 1834 they had moved to Paihia. Later, they moved to Waikare and then to the East Coast. Yate brought the first printing press to New Zealand in 1830, probably setting it up in the kitchen outhouse behind the mission house. His printing efforts were unsuccessful; only after the arrival of William Colenso in 1834 was the society able to print and distribute Māori translations of the Bible and other texts. William Yate briefly enjoyed the limelight of the CMS in the Bay, where he was initially considered the ideal man for the mission, 'the man we have wanted', according to Henry Williams, but after he was 'outed' as a homosexual in 1836, he suffered a complete fall from grace.

The missionaries' practice of 'redeeming' slaves continued. In June 1828, with the consent of everyone at the settlement, Kemp paid 'a chief' four blankets and one iron pot for a man who had spent the past two years as part of the Clarke household. His freedom was purchased as he wanted to marry a woman, herself redeemed from Hongi seven years earlier, who was a member of the Kemps' household. Yate drew up an agreement for the man's 'purchase'. The couple were to build a house within the settlement. Kemp noted that this was the second marriage linking the two households.

Links between the mission families were close. There was no medical expertise in the small community until the arrival of William Williams, brother of Henry, in 1826, and he was based at Paihia. Women depended on each other for assistance in childbirth and illness. All of the mission families at Kerikeri – the Kemps, Clarkes, Bakers and Hamlins – had increasing numbers of children during the 1820s. Babies were sometimes born only days

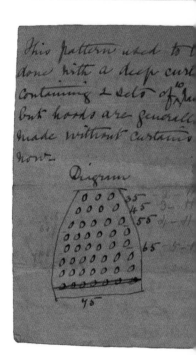

A knitting pattern for a 'Baby's Hood'.

Hand-stitched baby's gown,
Kemp House.

Collection of Kerikeri Mission Station © New Zealand Historic
Places Trust Pouhere Taonga

FIRST BAPTISMS

When Richard Cruise of the *Dromedary* visited the Bay in 1820, he mocked the missionaries as 'not a convert had yet been made'. After the Hohi mission was founded it was ten years before the CMS was able to celebrate the first conversion of a Māori to Christianity, at Paihia in 1824, when the chief 'Christian Rangi' was baptised on his deathbed. The baptism of Taiwhanga took place six years later, at the beginning of 1830, also at Paihia where he and his family then lived. On this occasion, the chief took the baptismal name Rawiri (David). Taiwhanga's children had been baptised the year before. No doubt John Butler's influence set Taiwhanga's conversion in place, but Henry Williams carried it out and took the credit for it.

Other conversions soon followed. Mere Taua (Meri Tawa) and her husband Hoani were among the first group of adults to be baptised at Kerikeri, on 26 September 1830. By the time of his death, even Tāreha had converted to Christianity. Rewa, living at Kororāreka from 1830, became more aligned with the Roman Catholic bishop, whose printing house and settlement stood close to Rewa's Ngāi Tāwake pa on the beachfront.

or weeks apart. Women at Kerikeri needed to be robust: James Kemp noted that Charlotte was 'naturally of a weak constitution' and unable 'to stand the fetague which females have to endure in this heathen land'. Later events proved him correct. Outbreaks of influenza, whooping cough and measles affected everyone, Māori and European. Missionaries remarked on the decrease in the Māori population because of these illnesses.

Charlotte Kemp gave birth to a fourth child in late January 1826, during an outbreak of what must have been influenza. At the time, Mrs Clarke was sick,

with a violent pain in the head, difficulty in breathing, and so weak as scarcely to be able to walk, this was a great trial for Mrs. Kemp, who was daily expecting to be confined, there being no other female that could be with her in the trying hour, in this settlement.

In July 1828, Martha Clarke gave birth to a daughter, but in June and August many of the children at Kerikeri, including the missionaries' own, were ill. October was still worse, 'a very sickly month' for both Māori and mission as an outbreak of whooping cough affected almost every child. The Clarkes' four-month-old daughter succumbed and died and was the first to be buried in the new burial ground on the hilltop, where construction of a new chapel was under way. Māori 'suffered much' from whooping cough, and many children were dying. Sometimes Kemp or Clarke made the journey to Waimate and back on foot in a single day to visit the sick with food and medicines, a distance of some thirty miles (nearly fifty kilometres).

Children's toys: a wooden Noah's ark and figurines in Kemp House.

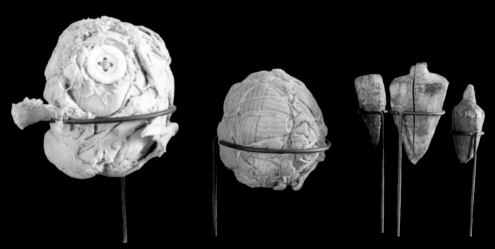

Children's toys recovered from beneath the floor at the Stone Store, which may have come from the boys' school held there in the 1860s: fabric and string balls, and three wooden pōtaka – a humming top, pōtaka tākiri (two examples at right); and a whip top, pōtaka tā (left).

Ceramic doll's head. This would have had a cloth body attached.

Collection of Kerikeri Mission Station © New Zealand Historic Places Trust Pouhere Taonga, XKH.3280

Cross-stitch pin cushion, probably made by a child.

Collection of Kerikeri Mission Station © New Zealand Historic Places Trust Pouhere Taonga, XKH.3275

A box of draughts pieces, ready for a game.

Collection of Kerikeri Mission Station © New Zealand Historic Places Trust Pouhere Taonga, XKH.3322

Within the mission settlement, missionary and Māori children grew up in the same households, played together and sometimes formed close relationships, as was the case with the eldest Clarke son, George, once a friend of Hone Heke, whose felling of the Kororāreka flagpole sparked the 1845 war with the British colonial government. By the age of four, the Kemp's eldest son Henry could read and write a little, and speak the Māori language very well. In his memoir, George Clarke recalled a childhood where 'fishing for sprats and eels seemed the noblest occupation of humanity'. Many of the mission 'servants' were rescued war slaves, protected and hidden inside the mission

Johny Heke + Wife.

Above: This school slate once belonged to Rongo Hongi, the daughter of Hongi Hika, as the inscription on the bottom shows. Rongo signed this with a nail, leaving permanent marks, and noted her age as sixteen years. After her baptism, Rongo took the name 'Hariata'. This slate was probably lost when James Kemp built the new kitchen in 1831; Rongo was living with the Kemp family at this time. It was uncovered during restoration work in 2000.

Collection of Kerikeri Mission Station © New Zealand Historic Places Trust Pouhere Taonga, XKH.3480

Above left: Hongi's daughter Hariata, with Hone Heke, painted by Joseph Jenner Merrett as *Johny Heke & Wife* (c. 1845).

National Library of New Zealand Te Puna Mātauranga o Aotearoa Alexander Turnbull Library, E-309-q-2-033

house from their former captors. Hongi once removed a young woman, a 'long time' servant of the Kemps, as a sailor had paid him a musket for her prostitution. As mentioned earlier, Māori of highest rank also entered the mission households, as did Rongo, Hongi's daughter, who took the baptismal name of Hariata. Hone Heke and Hariata Rongo married at the Kerikeri chapel in 1837.

George Clarke recalled a Māori population of many thousands living on either side of the Kerikeri Inlet during his childhood. He had an early 'dreamlike recollection' of being taken by his 'nurse' into Kororipo pā and Hongi taking him into his arms. At that time, Kororipo was full of houses. Clarke recalled an outer double stockade, with posts from fifteen to eighteen feet high and 'pits' – or more likely a ditch – between the stockades and a second ditch on the inside. (Others suggest that the pā was not palisaded at this time and that Clarke's recollections as an older man may have been incorrect.) In the centre of the stockade was the wharepuni, or chief's house. Clarke remembered, when no more than five years old, standing on the verandah of the mission

These bricks were made by Sydney convicts, whose thumb imprints are in the clay at the corners. James Kemp noted in his journal on 1 March 1831: 'With my natives moving some bricks from the wharf.'

Collection of Kerikeri Mission Station © New Zealand Historic Places Trust Pouhere Taonga, XKH.3609, XKH.3610

KEMP HOUSE OCCUPANTS

John and Hannah Butler, 1822–1823

(Marianne Williams stayed 6 weeks from August 1823)

James and Harriet Shepherd, 1823–1824

George and Martha Clarke, 1824–1830

(Hamlins stayed in March 1826)

(William Yate stayed in January 1828)

Thomas and Anne Chapman, 1831–1832

James and Charlotte Kemp, 1832–1870

(Charlotte died in 1860, James in 1872)

Kemp descendants, 1870–1974

house and 'watching the conflagration that consumed it all'. This was the fire that demolished Hongi's European house at the pā, torched by Tāreha in the middle of the night in September 1828, following his death on 6 March of that year. As a chief's house, the building was highly tapu and best destroyed.

Hongi, the fighting chief, was wounded in early 1827 in an attack on a tribe based at Whangaroa. A musket ball passed through his right lung and out near his spine. Although death appeared imminent, he pulled through this crisis. He returned to Kerikeri for occasional visits thereafter but remained unwell, and as he breathed, the air expelled through his right lung whistled. Hongi's death was finally reported in early March 1828. He died exhorting his people to be 'kind and affectionate to the praying Europeans'.

The mission's relationship with Māori changed after Hongi's death. Rewa, who had been second in line to Hongi, and his brother, Moka, became the principal chiefs connected with the Kerikeri mission, but in 1830 this altered again. Ngāpuhi politics in the Bay of Islands shifted as Rewa, Moka and their hapū, Ngāi Tāwake, took over the prime port in the Bay, Kororāreka, and Ngāti Manu, the Kororāreka people, relocated back up the harbour to the pā of Ōtūihu, opposite Opua, and their other lands near Kawakawa. In 1830, Kerikeri was also affected by the opening of the new mission station inland at Waimate, where Hongi had his gardens and once lived. The CMS now planned to develop its main farm at Waimate, where the land appeared promising for agriculture. The land was purchased from the chiefs also associated with Kerikeri – Rewa, Moka and Tāreha – it was their territory, located between the two impressive pā of Whakataha and Ōkuratope. In this sense, the Waimate mission could be considered an inland extension of Kerikeri. This was the place where Marsden had once promised Hongi he would create a farm. William Yate, the Clarkes and the Hamlins moved there in 1830.

Following the Clarke family's move to Waimate, a new mission family, Thomas and Anne Chapman, moved into the mission house on their arrival at Kerikeri in 1831. Thomas Chapman took on the role of storekeeper so that James Kemp could supervise the construction in stone of a new store, with the assistance of Charles Baker. And Anne Chapman took over the girls' school at Kerikeri.

After only a year, the Chapmans and the Kemps swapped houses, beginning the long Kemp family tenure of the mission house that lasted into the mid-twentieth century. In 1833, the Chapmans moved to Paihia and James and Harriet Shepherd and their family moved from Te Puna (the mission that replaced Hohi in 1832, where they were stationed with John King and his

Above, left and right: Charlotte and James Kemp. Charlotte may be holding a pair of spectacles in her hand.

Collection of Kerikeri Mission Station © New Zealand Historic Places Trust Pouhere Taonga, XKH.3652 and XKH.3653

Left: Writing desk and spectacles (inset), Kemp House. In April 1839 Kemp's order to London included a request for '2 pr. Silver Speticales for woman 50 years of age, with spare glasses'.

Collection of Kerikeri Mission Station © New Zealand Historic Places Trust Pouhere Taonga, XKH.2608 (desk)

Right: The Kemp House kitchen, reconstructed in 2000, possibly using the Butler/Kemp family fire crane and other equipment.

Collection of Kerikeri Mission Station © New Zealand Historic Places Trust Pouhere Taonga

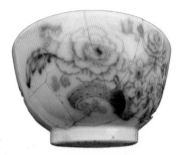

Above: An underglaze transfer-printed bowl, found beneath the floor of Kemp House near the northern chimney.

Collection of Kerikeri Mission Station © New Zealand Historic Places Trust Pouhere Taonga, XSS 666

Left: Fragments of a small bowl found during archaeological investigations of the Kemp House verandah garden bed in 2000. They show the transfer ware pattern known as 'Grazing Rabbits'. Fragments of a similar bowl of the same pattern were found beneath the floor of the house, also in 2000.

Collection of Kerikeri Mission Station © New Zealand Historic Places Trust Pouhere Taonga, XSS.904

family) back to Kerikeri, where James became storekeeper until 1836. Later in this year, after the Stone Store was completed, Kemp took over again. John Edmonds, the stonemason who came to complete the Stone Store, also remained along with his wife and five children, building a stone house on his land on the Kerikeri Inlet and moving there in 1839.

Changes to the mission house came with the Kemps' occupancy. In 1832, James Kemp began the construction of a lean-to at the rear of the house, which consisted of five rooms. Up until this date, the house was simply one room in width, as shown in Butler's plan of 1820. The southern end of the lean-to was first to be built and extended; Kemp was again working on the lean-to in 1834. The indoor kitchen may have been completed at this time, as the old outdoor kitchen had already been demolished, probably in 1831 when the new blacksmith shop was built (see Chapter 4). Before the old kitchen was demolished, it may have housed Yate's printing press. In about 1842 or 1843 the original verandah was replaced, with north and south returns added which ran up to the

lean-to at the rear. This remodelling removed the original rooms from each end of the verandah.

While the population at the kāinga had decreased, Kerikeri still provided access to the sea and coastal resources to those people living inland at Waimate and Taiamai. With the Stone Store completed, Kemp resumed his former occupations of storekeeper and itinerating missionary, visiting villages around the Bay of Islands and along the coast to the north. Over one thousand Māori were visited from Kerikeri, and they were anxious to have schools established in their areas.

Schooling continued at Kerikeri. Charlotte Kemp managed to teach the 'Native Girls School' at the mission house for a part of each day, despite pregnancies, childbirth and illness. Her eighth child, Samuel, was born in October 1834 and the last, a daughter named after her mother, was born in 1838, when Charlotte was forty-eight and James forty-one. The death of Samuel on 28 May 1835 had serious consequences. James Kemp reported that he was unable to carry on his usual visits to villages around the Bay, due to Charlotte's 'affliction' – mental illness – 'her mind being so affected, it was not prudent for me to leave home'. Charlotte needed her husband's constant attention.

Within a few months, Charlotte Kemp recovered sufficiently to resume teaching the girls' school, although intermittent bouts of mental breakdown recurred throughout the rest of her life. Mere Taua, also known as Mary Tawa, was teaching the infants' school. Mere's husband John also taught in the school; he died in December 1836 'after a lingering illness', by which time he had

Kerikeri in the late nineteenth century, showing Kemp House with the 1843 verandah and blacksmith shop at the rear. The Stone Store is at the left.

Hocken Collections Uare Taoka o Hakena, University of Otago, S12-598e

Kerikeri Mission House (Kemp House),
south elevation, 2003.

lived with the Kemps for some sixteen years. Mere continued
to teach, with her pupils in the infant class usually numbering
around ten or twelve, until her death in 1848. Henry, the eldest
Kemp son, who spoke Māori well, was sent back to England in
1834. When he returned in August 1837, he assisted his father
with the stores, writing up the accounts and ledgers and teaching
school on the 'Sabbath'. From mid-1838, his sister Elizabeth, then
aged about fifteen, 'lame and of a weak constitution' (it is likely
Elizabeth's lameness was caused by polio), joined her mother in
teaching the girls' school.

With the development of the Paihia and Waimate stations,
the Kerikeri mission became less important as a CMS hub in the
Bay of Islands. In 1839, James Shepherd and his family shifted
to Whangaroa, where he established a 'branch' mission at the
request of Hongi's son. He made this move reluctantly, as Harriet
Shepherd's mental state was precarious: they had made thirteen
moves in the same number of years. This left the Kemps as the
single mission family at Kerikeri.

Kemp House: interior and items from its collections, 2013.

All images collection of Kerikeri Mission Station © New Zealand Historic Places Trust Pouhere Taonga

1.

2.

3.

7.

1–3. Upstairs back bedroom; Child's dolls and teddies; Child's bed, book (*Life of Christ*) and wall.

4. Child's bedroom wall, papered with pages from the *Illustrated London News*, with articles on (left) 'Chester Races May 9 1846' and (right) 'Burghley House North Front the Dinner Pavilion', also 1846.

5. Detail of a downstairs wall, papered with pages from a Māori dictionary or grammar.

6. Layers of mattresses on the child's bed.

7. Downstairs back bedroom.

8. The main upstairs bedroom (current configuration). This may have been the children's room in the 1830s and 1840s. A chair for nursing babies is next to the bed.

9. Detail of cushion on the nursing chair.

4. The Stone Store, 1836

By 1830 the wooden Kerikeri store, built in 1819, was in poor repair – in fact rotten – and needed to be replaced. Deciding how to do this was no simple matter in the political world of the Bay of Islands missionaries, where each argued for the benefits of their own station.

Initially the local committee passed a resolution to move the CMS store to Paihia, closer to the shipping in the deeper part of the harbour. Henry Williams in particular supported this and even the storekeeper James Kemp approved the move. However, wider CMS developments meant that this plan did not proceed. In 1830, Marsden returned to the Bay and the decision was made to establish the Waimate mission as a farming centre. Wheat grown there would be transported along a road that would be built from Waimate to Kerikeri, where Marsden had long planned a flourmill would operate. A new store at Paihia would not work; it was too far from Waimate.

When George Clarke, Rev. William Yate and James Hamlin moved to the new Waimate station with their families in mid-1830, the case for a new store at Kerikeri was revived. James Kemp drew up a simple plan for a two-storey stone building, 50 feet by 30 feet, that the committee approved. Henry Williams was not appeased, but Marsden carried the decision for Kerikeri. A stone building would be similar, in solidity, permanence and appearance, to English warehouses. It also offered the benefit of fire resistance. Wesleyan John Hobbs subsequently produced more substantial plans for a building of two storeys, with an attic third floor and dormer windows.

A 'runner stone' from a domestic hand mill for grinding flour and corn. This example was found on a terrace beside the river to the north of Kemp House in 1998, probably placed there to form part of a path by Gertrude and Charlotte Kemp, who used mill stones for this purpose.

Marsden's long-planned mill did not proceed. Mill-builder Kinghorne came from New South Wales and drew up plans for the mill to be erected alongside the store. After his departure, leaving directions for work to be undertaken, the idea was scuttled. The missionaries realised that the tidal nature of the inlet, along with the threat of flooding, meant that the mill would not operate effectively. Instead, a mill was erected at Waimate in 1834 to grind the mission flour.

Stonemason William Parrott, a former convict, arrived with his family from New South Wales in October 1831 to begin building, under the supervision of James Kemp. Basalt from further down the Kerikeri Inlet was the basic building material but sandstone was brought from New South Wales for more decorative elements such as quoins, jambs and archstones. Parrott began cutting the stone immediately after his arrival and by May 1832 had laid the foundations. Shell to use as mortar was burnt for lime and stored near the site. People from the kāinga assisted with all these tasks. A new blacksmith shop was also built at the back of the mission house, where by this time Kemp and his family lived, so that Kemp could work on the fittings for the new store. Carpenter James Nesbit (Nisbet/Nesbet) came from Port Jackson to work on the building as well, and a carpenters' workshop was constructed for him and his assistants. Unfortunately there are no known sketches of what must have been a scene of much industry.

By March 1834 the roof framing of the store was finished, and it was nearly ready for shingling. Having completed the walls of the store, William Parrott left for Whangaroa, where he

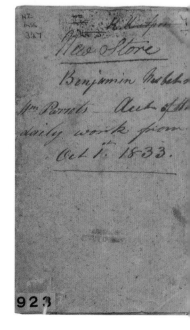

JAMES KEMP REPORTS ON PROGRESS

Report, 7 October 1833.

Benjamin Nesbet Carpenter employed during the past quarter, framing frist [sic] floor of joists finished making sashes & window frames & doors for new store have commenced framing roof for the same.
Wm. Parrot Stone mason, most of the last quarter employed in cutting free stone for window head & jambs, the last fortnight employed in building the walls of the store.

Report, 7 January 1834.

Wm. Parrot Stone mason employed building the walls of the store he hopes to finish the walls in about six weeks or two months from this time. Benjamin Nesbet carpenter employed during framing the roof for the store & has got it about three parts done, he has also laid the first floor of joists and repeard the punt.

Kemp's record of William Parrott's 'Daily Work on the Stone Store', April–June 1832. Notable events include: 9 May, 'Laid the foundation stone'; 10 May, 'out shooting'; 12 June, 'His wife confined'.

Auckland Public Library, 7–C1884

Kemp's account book for carpenter Nesbit's and stonemason Parrott's daily work on the Stone Store, from 1 October 1833.

Auckland Public Library, 7–C1884

settled near William Spikeman, another former NSW convict associated with the CMS. The CMS in London now sent a second stonemason, John Edmonds who took over construction of the store. The framed roof was altered in May 1834 to accommodate a bell tower, a variation on the original plan. The mission's clock and bell were housed in the tower, on the southwest corner of the store; a weathercock was placed on top of the copper roof.

George Clarke, James Hamlin and Richard Davis (another lay missionary) built the Waimate–Kerikeri road and a bridge across the Waitangi River in 1830. At Kerikeri, Edmonds built a new stone pier and a road leading to it, cutting through the hill behind the mission station to join the Waimate road. This road cutting destroyed the site of the first chapel/school, demolished in 1828 when the first church on the current site (where St James Church stands today) was built and completed in 1829.

The impressive Stone Store, the CMS's most expensive venture to date, was ready to receive the mission goods for storage in early 1835. By this time it was almost redundant, for the society was debating whether the Kerikeri mission was sustainable. Henry Williams, chairman of the local committee, wanted it closed; Kemp defended the store, arguing that it had been erected 'at a very great expense to the Society'. The mission committee eventually decided in favour of retaining Kerikeri. The stone building still needed to be finished: the roof completed, two upper floors to be laid, and windows and doors installed. River-worn basalt cobblestones were used for the ground floor, while in the small room on the north side a wooden floor was laid on top of the stones. Māori workers shingled the roof, and Kemp made the required ironwork and glazed the new windows. The staircase was not completed until mid-1836. Nesbit then finished off the 'projecting part' of the roof and built internal partitions and shelving. Having finished

EARLY SKETCHES OF THE STONE STORE

CMS missionary Richard Taylor, a prolific artist, worked in the Bay of Islands between 1839 and 1843. He took time to sketch the mission station at Kerikeri. The top sketch was drawn from Kororipo or the ridge leading to the pā, and shows the Stone Store with the bell tower and original dormer windows; the date 'Augst 9 1841' can be seen in the lower left-hand corner. The store built in 1819 can be seen at the far left, while on the hill above is the 1829 church (replaced with the current building in 1878). Beside that is the old Baker/Edmonds house, surrounded by vegetation. The small house beside the road, opposite the store, may be that of stonemason William Parrott while he worked on the store. National Library of New Zealand Te Puna Mātauranga o Aotearoa, Alexander Turnbull Library, E-296-q-035-1

The second drawing (below) is undated and gives a view of Kerikeri from the church hill behind the station. On the left is the Stone Store, while on the right the mission's first buildings can be seen: the old store, and the houses occupied by the Butters, Kemps and Francis Hall. Across the river is the headland of Kororipo pā and the ridge that led to the kāinga. National Library of New Zealand Te Puna Mātauranga o Aotearoa, Alexander Turnbull Library, E-296-q-035-3

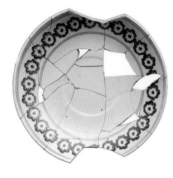

China saucers with sponged decoration found during archaeological work at the Stone Store.

Collection of Kerikeri Mission Station © New Zealand Historic Places Trust Pouhere Taonga, XSS.925 (larger saucer), XSS.583 (smaller saucer)

the store, he made a 'Shower bath' for the settlement, undoubtedly an innovation; it is unclear whether this was attached to the store or the mission house.

What were the goods that went into the Stone Store on its completion? It is possible to detail these from the accounts kept by James Kemp. In the late 1830s his sons Henry and James junior assisted him in the store. The goods they ordered and issued began to vary in kind and expand in quantity, although the standard fabrics and hardware remained. On Kemp's personal account in 1836, he ordered ready-made clothing for his family, including '6 Printed dresses', two each for his daughters, aged fifteen, twelve and seven, 'to be made large with tucks and full in every way'. He was apparently allowing for growth and economy. The same order included four dozen 'Women's striped cotton Shifts', 'stays' for his two eldest daughters and twelve 'Large Mens Calico Drawers' – the first time such articles of underclothing appear. While James Shepherd made his own shoes, the Kemp family did not. Strong, heavy-wearing shoes may have been a problem in Kerikeri, given the long distances James Kemp had to walk. In 1837, he sent an order to London for a total of fifty-five pairs of shoes, of lengths varying from 7½ inches to 12 inches, specifying whether these were to be 'light made' or 'fit for hard work'. Umbrellas also began to appear on goods orders, along with seeds for pasture, such as clover. Two years later, Kemp ordered another forty pairs of shoes from London, followed by another eighteen pairs. Fashion may have overcome some practicality by then. Some of the 'Ladies' and girls' shoes were to be of 'mock kid', the woman's to be 'very broad'. 'Wellington boots' also appeared in the books for the first time.

When James Shepherd departed for Whangaroa in 1839, the Kemps remained at Kerikeri as the only mission family. However, the signing of the Te Tiriti o Waitangi (Treaty of Waitangi) in February 1840 created a burgeoning settler population. The role of the CMS in northern New Zealand began to change and, as had been argued in 1835, the Stone Store was no longer an essential part of mission life in the Bay of Islands.

The mission committee voted to dispense with its public store in 1842. In the same year, the building was rented to the recently arrived Bishop George Selwyn and his wife Sarah. The Selwyns lived at Waimate, where the bishop established St John's College, but the bishop's valuable library was housed at the store. In the room at the northern end of the first floor new shelves were installed for the books; the northern room on the ground floor was used as the Selwyns' 'retreat'.

The Selwyns had grand plans for this 'beautiful stone building' that they considered 'so utterly uncolonial' – such as retiring

Stone Store and Kemp House in 2003, when a road ran in front of the store.

Kerikeri Stone Store and wharf in the early twentieth century. The ridge where the kāinga once was is now bare. The cottage (far left) was built by Ebenezer Norris in 1860; the 1878 church stands on its present site on the hill.

Hocken Collections Uare Taoka o Hākena, University of Otago, S12-598f there to live in their old age – but, when the colonial government established after the signing of the Te Tiriti o Waitangi moved from the Bay of Islands to Auckland in 1841, it changed the fortunes of the north. In late 1844, when St John's College moved from Waimate to Auckland, the Selwyns and their books moved too and the store was redundant once more.

Oldest Stone Building in N.Z.
Keri Keri. Bay of Is. 19

5. Kerikeri
after 1840

Retrenchment of the New Zealand missions began in the 1840s, as the Church Missionary Society began the transition to a settler-focused Anglican Church under the leadership of Bishop Selwyn. The Kerikeri mission and the Stone Store were surplus to requirements; other settler stores operated around the Bay, particularly at Kororāreka, the favoured port for shipping, where Rewa and his hapū remained.

In the late 1840s, the local mission committee wanted the Kemps to shift to one of the newer southern missions. But James Kemp refused to budge as Charlotte was suffering a relapse of her former depression and mental disorder. He cited her age and ill health as reasons for remaining at Kerikeri and asked to be granted the mission house and a small portion of land. In 1849, his salary was reduced and retirement from the society followed in 1850. As a secular citizen, he continued much the same routines as before, visiting outlying villages, caring for the sick and taking services. He finally received title to the mission house in 1860, exchanged for thirteen acres of land at Kororipo. Charlotte Kemp had died several months earlier. James Kemp continued to have an interest in the operation of the store, where he initiated the kauri gum trade, until he shifted to Auckland to live with his eldest son, Henry Tacy Kemp, in about 1870. He died at his son's house in Grafton Road in February 1872 and was buried in the St Stephen's Church cemetery in Parnell.

Goods accumulated in the Stone Store and retained there during Bishop Selwyn's occupation were sold to Kemp's sons Richard and James in October 1843. They had been operating a store from the old Baker/Edmonds house and moved back to the Stone Store, leased to Richard, after the bishop's departure. A lease to Ebenezer Norris followed in 1857 and Norris married the youngest Kemp daughter, Charlotte, in 1859. In 1860, he built a cottage on part of the leased land, where the original mission buildings had stood, and where a restaurant is now located. John Edmonds, the stonemason who arrived in 1834 and finished the store, took it over briefly before his death in 1865.

Photograph of the 'blacksmithy', 2012. This building, although re-roofed, re-clad, and with new door and window joinery, may well be the remains of the first Kemp home, as comparison of the hipped-roof structures in this and the 1904 photograph (p. 63) demonstrates.

Under John Edmonds, the store weathered a reputation as a 'grog shop'. Although his preferred occupation was farming, James

Kemp junior took over the lease in 1864 and finally purchased the building from the CMS in 1874 for £500, although he did not receive the title for another nineteen years! The next storekeeper was James' son-in-law, John Black, an American married to James' daughter Ethel. During his lease the trade in kauri gum, first begun by James Kemp senior, continued, with the gum being sorted and graded on the store's first floor. Black also built a butcher's shop below the wharf.

Structural changes were made during these years. The clock was removed from the store tower in March 1844 (and taken to Waimate); the bell was taken to Rev. Maunsell's mission near the Waikato Heads in 1851. Some time before 1858 the bell tower and the dormer windows were also removed, the windows being replaced with skylights. The tall chimney on the northern wall was taken down in the late 1880s, probably because it was unsafe, and the original shingled roof was replaced with iron.

After James Kemp senior's death, the Kerikeri estate (land and mission house) passed first to his son, James, who died in 1899, and then to his great-grandson Ernest Kemp, son of Francis (or Frank) Kemp. Ernest Kemp's aunts, Gertrude and Charlotte, occupied Kemp House until Charlotte's death in 1940 and that of Gertrude in 1951. In 1926, a small bathroom and washhouse were added to the northern end of the lean-to: the only major addition or alteration to the mission house since the mid-1830s. Ernest Kemp moved into the house in 1954.

Ernest Kemp made further alterations to the store in the 1950s, replacing one of the windows in the northern wall with a door and building a concrete ramp outside this wall, part of a ramp that ran around three sides of the building. Early in 1974 he arranged for Kemp House to be endowed to the nation, transferred to the ownership of the New Zealand Historic Places Trust. His death followed in November that year. The trust purchased the Stone Store from the family estate in 1976.

During the years since the NZHPT's purchase of the Stone Store, some of the earlier modifications have been reversed. The iron roof was removed and replaced with shingles, and the dormer windows were reinstated. The northern and southern ramps have been removed, the window put back in the northern wall, and the eastern (entrance) ramp lowered to an earlier level. Other work has been carried out around the structure, removing the 'overburden' of the ground surface that had built up during the 170 years of the store's life. This restored the original ground surface and the drain built by the CMS at the west and south of the building. This had once kept the building free from moisture, but had been filled in over the years, resulting in 'rising damp' that threatened the structure. The chimney in the northern wall was also reinstated.

1906 view from the rear of the Kerikeri Mission House, with the old blacksmith shop (1831) at its rear and a small outhouse in the foreground. A small structure is visible on the site of Kororipo pā.

Auckland Public Library, 7-A4625 AWNS-19060104-p002-i001-x

1904 view of Kerikeri, with the cottage built by Ebenezer Norris in 1860 in the foreground (approximate site of the present restaurant), along with earlier mission buildings, including possibly the first Kemp home behind the cottage. The Stone Store is in the distance.

Auckland Public Library, AWNS-19041229-1-0-4

At the mission house, the bathroom and washhouse addition was removed, and the kitchen chimney and fireplace were rebuilt. NZHPT also built the curator's cottage (now partly a café) at the rear of the house, in approximately the same position as the 1831 blacksmith shop.

The strategic importance of Kerikeri and the protection Hongi had offered were the factors that made the place attractive to the Church Missionary Society in 1819. Kerikeri provided the agricultural land that Hohi did not, and it was also closer to the large inland Māori population at Waimate and Taiamai, setting the scene for the later mission at Waimate, a favourite plan of

Marsden's. More importantly, it was part of Hongi's fiefdom. Kororipo was the pā, the 'sea port', from which Ngāpuhi taua under Hongi and Rewa had moved south during the early 1820s. Under Hongi's protection, the Church Missionary Society consolidated its place in the Māori world as Kerikeri's role in the Bay of Islands economy grew in the 1820s, in the years before his death.

While Kororipo's population may have declined following the death of Hongi and again after Rewa, Moka and the hapū of Ngāi Tāwake moved their main residence to Kororāreka in 1830, the hapū's mana whenua at Kerikeri persisted. Kororipo and Kerikeri's importance as a political centre continued. In 1831, thirteen rangatira met at the pā to compose a letter to King William IV, affirming the relationship that Hongi had established with George IV in 1820 and requesting William's continuing alliance with Ngāpuhi. This was provoked by a report that the French were planning to colonise New Zealand. Similar political gatherings to deliberate over Ngāpuhi's relationship with Pākehā followed, such as the 1835 meeting at Waitangi to sign 'He Wakaputanga o te Rangatiratanga o Nu Tireni', the Declaration of Independence. The scribe for this document was Hare Hongi, who was educated at the Kerikeri mission. These gatherings among Ngāpuhi culminated in the event at Waitangi in early February 1840, when Te Tiriti o Waitangi was signed. Soon after this, in 1841, the seat of British government shifted from old Russell (Okiato) to Auckland, removing the heart of the Ngāpuhi trading economy into the territory of Ngāti Whatua, their longtime enemies. Economic decline in the north began.

Ngāpuhi (and wider Māori) dissatisfaction with the outcomes of the signing of Te Tiriti o Waitangi brought about further political deliberations. In March 1843, a great hākari was held at Kerikeri, with Rewa and Moka as hosts, to discuss the issue of land sales to the government and the disputed land at Ōruru (Doubtless Bay). The hākari was a traditional celebration or political gathering, where different iwi or hapū met and large quantities of food were displayed and then shared. Invited guests would usually reciprocate at a later date. On this occasion, a rectangular stage was erected south of the ridge leading to Kororipo, on a flat beside the Wairoa River, and its shelves were filled with nearly 2000 baskets of dried fish, an expression of the mana of the hosts.

Although by this time the pā was no longer occupied, Māori pupils continued to attend the mission school daily. Dissatisfaction grew about the outcome of Te Tiriti o Waitangi; Hōne Heke, the former mission protégé, led the resistance that erupted into the 1845 Northern War with the 'sacking' of Kororāreka. In May that year, British soldiers camped in the Stone Store and around the mission house on their way inland, where they were surprised

Hākari on the Wairoa River (detail), beyond Kororipo, 29 March 1843. Structures can be seen on the ridge at right rear, and are probably remnants of the Kerikeri kāinga. The figure sitting under the shelter on the Kororipo pā site (right) may be one of Bambridge's party and a black-clothed clergyman, possibly Henry Williams, is in the crowd.

National Library of New Zealand Te Puna Mātauranga o Aotearoa, Alexander Turnbull Library, William Bambridge, 1819–79: Diaries. MS-0130-021

Hākari held for Governor George Grey at Kororāreka, 1849.

National Library of Australia, Cuthbert Clarke, 1818–63, T2870 NK2004 LOC NZ31/H

to find there was no easy victory against Ngāpuhi in battles at Puketutu and Ōhaeawai. After peace was made in early 1846, Kerikeri was once again the place for deliberations and planning prior to the (reputedly) last Bay of Islands hākari, held at Kororāreka in 1849 for Governor George Grey. Large quantities of food were prepared at Kerikeri, then taken to Kororāreka and displayed on the massive stage, reported as being the largest-ever event of this kind.

By this date, James Kemp owned large areas of land at Kerikeri. In 1831, the society had purchased land known as the 'Children's Land', bought with the future of the Bay of Islands missions' children in mind. In 1838, Kemp additionally purchased the thirteen acres of Kororipo pā, which he later exchanged with the CMS for the title to Kemp House. In due course these (and other) pre-1840 land purchases were scrutinised by the Old Land Claims Commissioner, who ultimately gave title to Kemp and other mission families in a process that awarded absolute ownership to Europeans, despite the objections of Rewa and others, ignoring earlier indigenous (and missionary) understandings of overlapping use rights and mutual (non-exclusive) occupation. That first tenuous land transaction of 1819 had brought missionaries under the mana whenua of Ngāi Tāwake, under the controlling hand of Māori, but these first interactions also brought about a turning point. Some four decades later, Ngāi Tāwake no longer had land rights at Kerikeri, now a European farm and soon to be subdivided into a new settler township. The legitimacy of the large missionary land purchases in the Bay of Islands and beyond continues to be disputed.

Kerikeri basin from the air, May 2004. Kororipo pā is on the promontory in the centre, across the basin are the Stone Store and Kemp House. The kāinga was on the ridge running up to top left.

Kevin Jones, Department of Conservation

Glossary

hapū clan or subtribe
hākari a large gathering of iwi or hapū for feasting
iwi tribe
kāinga village
kauri, kahikatea, puriri types of native trees
kūmara sweet potato
mana prestige, authority
mana whenua territorial rights; power associated with the
    occupation of land
mere a short, flat weapon, often of greenstone
noa free from the restrictions of tapu
pā fortified Māori settlement
pākehā non-Māori, usually Caucasian
pōtaka spinning top
rangatira chief/s
raupo reed used as building material
taonga prized object/artefact
tapu sacred, restricted
taua war party
taua muru plundering party
toki hatchet
toki patiti short-handled hatchet
utu recompense
wharepuni chief's house
whata storage platform

Acknowledgements

Ngā mihi nui ki ngā tūpuna o Ngāpuhi nui tonu, especially those who once nurtured the Kerikeri mission and its inhabitants. The evidence of the relationship between Ngāpuhi and missionaries remains inscribed on the ground at Kerikeri and elsewhere in the Bay of Islands.

This book came about as part of a larger (forthcoming) project on the Bay of Islands, funded with a Claude McCarthy Fellowship and a Ministry for Culture and Heritage History Research Award for 2012. I am very grateful to these two organisations for the opportunity to undertake this research and writing – it has long been thought about. Many thanks to my referees, Charles Orser of Vanderbilt University, Nashville, and Helen Leach of the University of Otago, Dunedin, for their support in this.

My thanks also to the New Zealand Historic Places Trust for their assistance, in particular Rebecca Apperley and Priscilla Pitts from Wellington and the staff at the Kerikeri Mission House and Stone Store, who cheerfully dealt with my numerous intrusions to take photographs of objects in the collections. Thanks to Liz Bigwood, Bill Edwards and Stuart Park for their local knowledge and support, and to Milly Harris-Webb and Debbie McKechnie, among others.

I am also grateful to others who have assisted: Cath Fergusson, of Kerikeri, for information about Tamihanga Maitarahanga, also known as Tutu; to those who presented papers at the Tauiwi/ Iwi Christianity conference at Waitangi in November 2012, for providing some small but significant missing details; to Pat Baskett for reading and commenting on drafts; to Ian Smith, for being a ready source of support and intellectual engagement, for reading drafts, and for producing the map on page 5.

Thank you to the organisations that have given reproduction rights for various images: the Mitchell and Dixson Libraries from the State Library of New South Wales, Australia; the Alexander Turnbull Library, Wellington; the Auckland Public Library; and the Hocken Collections, University of Otago, Dunedin. And especially thanks to Wendy Harrex, former publisher of Otago University Press, who envisioned this specific Kerikeri book when it was still only gestating as part of the wider research.

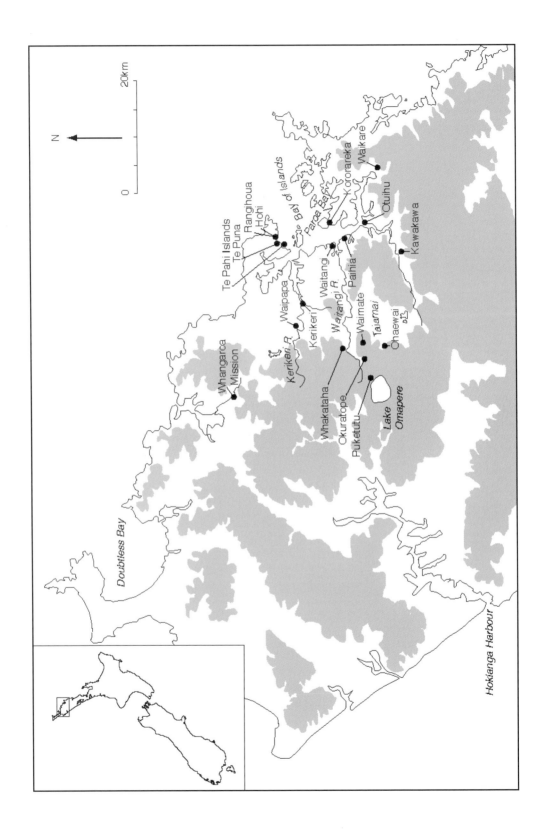

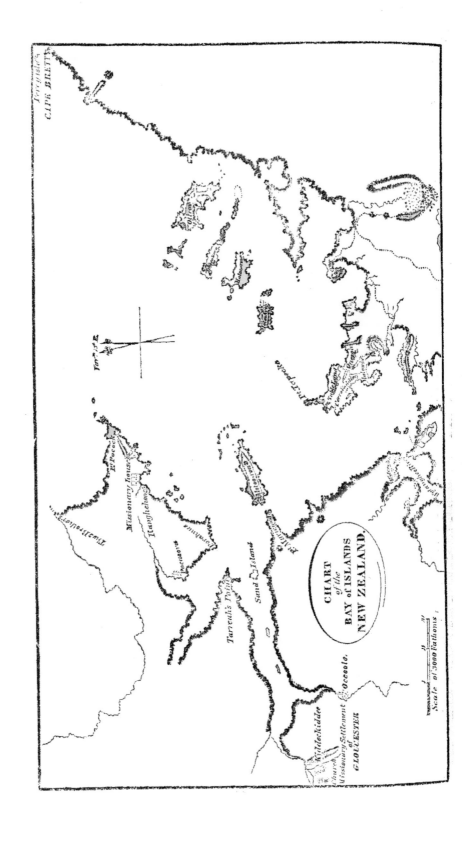

CHART
of the
BAY of ISLANDS
NEW ZEALAND.

Scale of 3000 Fathoms

Further Reading

John Barton, *Earliest New Zealand* (Masterton: Palamontain & Petherick, 1927).

Judith Binney, *Te Kerikeri 1770–1850: The meeting pool* (Wellington: Bridget Williams Books, 2007)

Judith Binney, *The Legacy of Guilt: A life of Thomas Kendall* (Wellington: Bridget Williams Books, 2005)

M. Campbell, L. Furey & S. Holdaway, *Finding Our Recent Past: Historical archaeology in New Zealand* (Auckland: NZ Archaeological Association, 2013)

George Clarke jnr, *Notes on Early Life in New Zealand* (Hobart: J. Walch, 1903; Christchurch: Cadsonbury Publications, 2008)

Dorothy Urlich Cloher, *Hongi Hika: Warrior chief* (Auckland: Viking 2003)

Nola Easdale, *Missionary and Maori* (Lincoln: Te Waihora Press, 1991)

J.R. Elder, *The Letters and Journals of Samuel Marsden, 1765–1838* (Dunedin: Coulls Somerville Wilkie & A.H. Reed for Otago University Council, 1932)

J.R. Elder, *Marsden's Lieutenants* (Dunedin: Coulls Somerville Wilkie & A.H. Reed for Otago University Council, 1934)

Caroline Fitzgerald, *Letters from the Bay of Islands* (Auckland: Penguin, 2004)

Alison Jones and Kuini Jenkins, *He Kōrero / Words Between Us: First Māori–Pākehā conversations on paper* (Wellington: Huia Publishers, 2011)

Angela Middleton, *Te Puna: A New Zealand mission station* (New York: Springer, 2008)

Jeffrey Sissons, Wiremu Wi Hongi and Pat Hohepa, *Ngā Pūriri o Taiamai* (Auckland: Reed Publishing, 2001)

Index

Page numbers in **bold** refer to illustrations.